LIFE'S PUNCHLINES
A Poetic Memoir of a Milestone Junkie

Mayette Lerin Pastrano

ISBN   978-1-966473-46-6 Ebook
ISBN   978-1-966473-45-9 Paperback

The EC Publishing LLC books may be ordered through booksellers or by contacting:

EC Publishing LLC
116 South Magnolia Ave.
Suite 3, Unit F
Ocala, FL 34471, USA
Direct Line: +1 (352) 644-6538
Fax: +1 (800) 483-1813
http://www.ecpublishingllc.com/

Ordering Information:
Quantity sales. Special discounts are available on quantity purchases by corporations, associations, and others. For details, contact the publisher at the address above.

Printed in the United States of America

Table of Contents

Dedication

To my family — my guiding stars, my ever-beating
heart, my compass and my radiant dawn ...
You are the reason I dare to dream, to strive, to
chase the horizon and cherish every milestone.
You give me the strength to brave the unknown,
and find home on every uncharted road.

To every soul who has graced my path ...
Friends, mentors, silent witnesses, kindred spirits,
and even fleeting encounters — thank you for
lending your hues to the canvas of my journey,
for shaping the crude masterpiece that is me.

This book is for all of us who've ever felt like we're
just winging it but somehow still manage to soar ...

a testament to the beautiful chaos of life;
a tribute to the courage that lifts fragile wings;
and a reminder that even broken flight is still flight.

Prologue: The Milestone Junkie's Manifesto

I'm a milestone addict. There, I said it. I crave those markers of progress like a kid craves candy. Birthdays, graduations, the first day of school, learning to play the piano —bring 'em on! I'll take a milestone any way I can get it, even if it's a made-up one like "National Learn to Just Say No Day" (which, by the way, is every day for me).

You see, I believe the end of our journey is inevitable. It'll come whether we like it or not. But the milestones? Those are the good stuff—the sprinkles on the sundae of life, the punchlines to the cosmic jokes we call "living."

The milestones are what make up a life. They're the measure of how we live our days. They're the proof that we're making progress, even if it's one wobbly step at a time and even when we feel we aren't making any. And it makes the long haul of waiting on a long-term goal so much easier and happier! Who wouldn't want any excuse to have a party or to get in a good crying session over the multitude of life dramas your hormones want you to deal with, right?

So, in these pages, you'll find my love letters to the milestones that have shaped me—the ones that made me laugh, cry, and everything in between. From the mundane to the monumental, I've learned that every milestone has a lesson to teach us if we're willing to listen.

So, join me, fellow milestone junkies, as we celebrate the highs, commiserate the lows, and find the humor in it all. Because let's be real — if we can't laugh at ourselves, who can we laugh at? (Hint: no one. The answer is no one.)

Life's punchlines await. Let's dive in, shall we?

Chapter 1

The miracle of happenstance reveals itself in hindsight, winking at us as we realize that every twist and turn was just the universe's way of keeping things interesting, serving up surprises we never saw coming.

Why do we have this relentless urge to justify everything we do, especially when life is a wild rollercoaster ride that we can't control? Is it our chronic indecision or our desperate need for a backup excuse in case things go south? You know, so we can point fingers and say, 'It wasn't me, it was the universe!'

Did I have a grand master plan for getting married at 21? Not really... although I suspect that the six-year age gap with my then-boyfriend of four years might have played a cheeky role in this delightful twist of fate. In retrospect, I did make a rather bold proclamation at the ripe old age of 5 — one I completely forgot about until after my wedding — declaring that since my mother got hitched at 20, I would one-up her by saying 'I do' on my 21st. Who would've guessed that a whimsical childhood daydream would magically manifest and lead me down the aisle instead of swinging on the playground? So, a word of caution: Be careful what you wish for because the universe is always eavesdropping and might just decide to grant your request!

Did I see myself at 23 years old when we started planning to have children that I'd be cranking out three kids in under three years? Not specifically! And did I ever think I'd trade years of hard-earned study, a shiny board exam license, a master's degree, and a promising career for the glamorous life of a full-time teacher, secretary, driver, and nanny to my husband and kids? Ha! Not in a million years!

But here I am, folks—life threw me a curveball, and I'm just here trying to catch it with one hand while juggling laundry and diapers with the other. It just happened! That's my story— and I'm sticking to it! Life made me do it, and honestly, I'm still trying to figure out how I ended up in this sitcom episode I never auditioned for. Everything just fell into place by chance, like a cosmic game of Tetris gone wonderfully awry!

At first, I was like a dog chasing its tail, overwhelmed by the whirlwind of my new reality. Lost time? Check! Missed opportunities? Double-check! What is life without a little melodrama, right? Yet, as the dust settled and emotions calmed, I began to see the miracle of happenstance. There's a certain thrill in the unplanned, a rush that comes with the realization that life is a series of blessed milestones cloaked in the form of Happen chances.

Looking back, I am grateful for my early start. It has led me to a beautiful relationship with my three daughters, who have become my best friends. The gift of being a full-time mother and wife is one I cherish, despite the challenges that come with it. Sure, there were years when I felt like I was battling the repercussions of my choices, grappling with a seemingly lost sense of self. I often wondered if I had bartered my above-average IQ and lofty career goals for a life of baby baths, feedings, and diaper changes— essentially earning a degree in 'Toddler Studies' with a specialization in 'Nap time Negotiations!' And let me tell you, those extra servings on my stomach, hips, and thighs can make you feel like you're losing not just your figure but your sanity too—thanks to the delightful mayhem that hormones gone wild can bring!

But here's the kicker: I wouldn't trade this life for anything. In a million years and a million lifetimes over, I would not live my life any other way...

The miracle of happenstance reveals itself in the most unexpected ways, like finding a 1000 bill in the pocket of a pair of jeans you haven't worn since the last Ice Age. I assure myself of a regret-free existence by pouring my heart and soul into every choice I make when life allows me to have one. When you chase what you love, surrounded by the people who matter most, nothing else really matters—not even when happenstance wields its might and life decides to throw you a pie in the face.

So, what's the game plan when life serves you a heaping plate of unpredictability? You become the kind of person who can turn a disaster into a smashing sold-out comedy show, making the most out of whatever life pushes you into, whether it's a gentle nudge or a full-on shove.

Just because life is one big, chaotic circus doesn't mean we can't grab some popcorn and enjoy the spectacle!

A Milestone Junkie's Prayer

Dear life, grant me strength today,
To embrace every milestone, come what may!
In giggles and snorts, may I find grace,
Tackling each challenge with
a smile on my face!

Guide me through sunshine and rain,
Help me find sparkle, even in pain.
With each mini-win, let my spirit soar,
Show me the wisdom that
moments have in store!

Grant me the wisdom to learn from my slips,
The strength to bounce back
from life's little dips.
In gratitude, I'll hold each memory dear,
For every milestone, whispers,
"You're still here."

Chapter 2

*In life's grand theater, we trade sacrifices for
joy, for every breathtaking performance is
born from relentless backstage hustle ...
reminding us that joy is often the
radiant spotlight illuminating our
hardest battles.*

So, I might have mentioned that I'd happily live this life over again in a million lifetimes. What I conveniently left out is that it took an entire circus of pandemonium to get me here! Ah, the countless bawl fests on our bedroom floor, triggered by landline phones ringing — those pesky calls I couldn't answer because I was woefully short an extra pair of hands in a world where speakerphones were sci-fi fantasy! It felt like the phones were mocking me: "Go ahead, pick me up if you can!"

And let's not even talk about those "I-desperately-need-a-bath" days when my ponytail decides to go rogue and stubbornly flops dramatically to one side of my head despite all my efforts to straighten it. Meanwhile, sweat and spilled milk would form an unholy alliance, always congregating in that special spot where my aching boobs met my still-bulging, now-fake pregnant belly. Honestly, it was like a mini swamp down there!

But wait, there's more! Picture this: my eldest daughter, barely three years old, is perched in the playpen, doubling as her nighttime bed next to mine like a tiny queen surveying her kingdom. On my left, my spirited two-year-old is wedged between me and the playpen wall to keep her from falling. And on my right? An infant who seems to have taken up permanent residence latched to my breast like it's the coziest VIP lounge in town— this, all night, every night. Believe me when I say I was the reigning queen of multitasking!

Just when I think I might catch a break, the baby cries out, signaling it's time for a diaper change. This triggers the still-a-baby older sister to join in with a full-on toddler tantrum that could rival any Broadway musical. Meanwhile, I'm the hapless mother performing a mad dash for nappy clean-up, trying to calm the chaos before it spirals into a full-blown symphony of wails that would make even the most seasoned conductor weep.

In that moment, I'm juggling emotions like flaming torches — frustration flares up as I wonder if I'll ever see the bathroom again, quickly followed by an adrenaline-fueled guilt that made me feel like the worst mother in the world for having feelings of walking out while questioning every life choice I've ever made — like why I thought having three kids was a good idea! This was partnered with an overwhelming urge to join in on the cacophony of cries echoing around me. And just when I thought I might lose it completely, I suddenly burst into fits of laughter at the sheer absurdity of it all—if only someone could see me in those moments! This scene was pure comedy gold, and I was the star of my own slapstick show!

Day in and day out, my life felt like a never-ending rollercoaster ride—complete with dizzying highs, stomach-dropping lows, and the occasional loop-de-loop that left me breathless. My body had spawned three little bodies in less than three years, all while I was surviving on a mere 2-3 hours of sleep daily (that's a total in that 24-hour period, mind you!). It was a recipe for disaster!

I found myself wrestling with the worst kind of postpartum depression. It got so bad after my third baby that I'd literally have to pick myself up from the floor after bouts of wailing that could rival any dramatic soap opera (over some random TV ad, I can't even remember what about).

Somewhere in moments of seeming lucidity, I realized I didn't even know what I was crying about! Was it my inability to squeeze into any of my non-maternity clothes, which now seemed to mock me from the depths of my closet like cruel little ghosts of fashion past? Or perhaps it was the near-empty refrigerator that looked like it had been abandoned by a family of starving college students — restocking it felt like a task destined for the next million years, assuming I could find time between diaper changes and toddler tantrums. And let's not forget my hair, which had taken on a life of its own and was staging an all-out rebellion against any form of styling.

Even my trips to our family doctor for routine check-ups turned into marathon talk sessions (with me doing most of the talking of just about anything!)—sometimes an hour long or more—where we'd have heartfelt conversations (bless her heart for patiently listening while I spilled my emotional spaghetti all over her office). Little did I know, I was wearing my depression like a neon sign flashing "Help Wanted!"

It was during one particularly tearful visit that I had to muster every ounce of strength to admit I needed help when she brought it up. It felt like admitting defeat in a game where the rules kept changing. At that moment, nothing less than professional help would suffice. So, with all the grace of a toddler attempting to walk in oversized shoes, I made the call to schedule an appointment with a psychiatrist.

In a daze and with my brain's instinct for self-preservation kicking in, I drove myself to the doctor's office. The car ride felt surreal like I was on autopilot while my mind raced with questions. What would this doctor be like? Would it be like a movie scene where I get to lie on a comfy couch and talk all my depression away? Or would it be a lumpy old sofa that smelled funny? And most importantly, would they have snacks? (I was really hoping for chocolate.)

I felt like I was on my way to somewhere as taboo as sneaking into a secret speakeasy during Prohibition. The thought of going to a psychiatrist felt like I was about to confess my deepest, darkest secrets to a room full of judgmental American Idol judges for the world to watch. It was the kind of thing you whispered about in hushed tones, as if I were heading to a clandestine meeting where the password was "I need help." Back then, in our little city in the South, seeking professional help could easily earn you a one-way ticket to Crazy Town, and nobody wanted to wear that badge of honor. So you can imagine that was BIG for me to be doing so!

When I finally plopped down in that waiting room, surrounded by posters about mental health and pamphlets that promised hope, something inside me shifted. My body, heart, and soul would forever be grateful for that difficult milestone moment — the one that took me from being a complete wreck to a work in progress. It wasn't instant magic; it was more like slow-cooked Binignit—rich and flavorful but needing time to simmer and the occasional stir to keep from burning.

As I navigated this winding road toward healing, I discovered that vulnerability wasn't weakness but strength wrapped in authenticity. While I still had days where tears flowed freely and frustration bubbled up like an overcooked pot of pasta, there were also days filled with laughter—laughter that echoed through our home and reminded me that even amidst all the crazy, joy could thrive.

For over a year, I embarked on this journey to reclaim my physical, emotional, and mental health. I faithfully attended my therapy sessions and took the medicine I was prescribed, like clockwork. And I started exercising again. Never in a million years did I imagine finding myself in this situation, but life had other plans, and I knew I had to embrace it if it meant bringing back the mother my daughters deserved.

Some days felt exhausting and daunting yet, amidst all the chaos, there were those little moments of clarity, tiny bursts of joy that reminded me I was still here...and that one day, maybe, hopefully soon, I would be "Me" again.

Yetti's Lullaby

(Verse 1)
Hush now, my darling, the stars softly gleam,
In the quiet of night, I'll hold you tight in my dreams.
Though shadows linger and dark clouds may appear,
I'm fighting my battles to find my
way back to you, my dear.

(Chorus)

Lullaby, sweet child, close your eyes tight,
Mama's here beside you through the dark of the night.
With each gentle whisper, I'll mend what is torn,
For you need your mother, I'll be here till the morn.

(Verse 2)
The weight feels heavy, like stones on my chest,
But your laughter is sunlight; it brings me my rest.
I'll gather my courage; I'll chase off the gray,
For your smiles are the reason I'm finding my way.

Lullaby, sweet child, close your eyes tight,
Mama's here beside you through the dark of the night.
With each gentle whisper, I'll mend what is torn,
For you need your mother, I'll be here till the morn.

So sleep now, my darling; let worries take flight,
I'm learning to shine again; I promise we'll be alright.

Chapter 3

When doubt's shadow falls, resilience
whispers— 'Game on!'
Time to show the world what you're
forged from!

I t all began when I was 26 — a young mom wrangling three tiny tornadoes aged 2, 1, and a mere 3 months. Picture me, juggling diapers and snack time, blissfully unaware that I was about to embark on an eight-year odyssey worthy of its own reality show!

Little did I know, my journey would include a million tests, a cast of ear, brain, and even psych doctors (yes, I was told I might be imagining my symptoms—because who wouldn't want to hallucinate about their health?). There were month-long episodes of being bedridden that made me feel like I was auditioning for the role of "Professional Couch Potato."

At one point, in a fit of desperation and sleep deprivation, I begged my husband to ask my doctor if they could just induce a coma—just for a little R&R! Finally, after what felt like an eternity of medical mysteries, the verdict arrived: SUPERIOR CANAL DEHISCENCE SYNDROME. Yes, folks, it sounds as fancy as it is confusing!

In layman's terms, I had a charming little hole in the bone that separated my ear canal from my brain—who doesn't love a surprise feature like that?! This delightful anomaly unleashed a bizarre bundle of symptoms that flipped my world upside down like a pancake on a Sunday morning. It felt like my life hit the pause button while I was stuck in an endless loop of confusion and chaos. The only cure? An experimental surgery performed less than ten times abroad at that time because by then, the syndrome had also been just discovered around the same time I started feeling the symptoms — talk about exclusive! No wonder the doctors in the Philippines couldn't figure out what was wrong for eight looong years; they were still trying to untangle the mystery like it was a particularly stubborn pair of wired earphones!

Fast forward to my early 30s, and reality hit me like a ton of bricks! I realized I might never get to do all those wild dreams I had scribbled on napkins during late-night snack sessions. Faced with the choice between high-risk brain surgery in the States (which felt about as appealing as skydiving without a parachute) or accepting my limitations and just living with it so I can be around for my little ones, I decided to embrace Plan B: the art of living with a quirky twist!

But guess what? Over 20 years passed, and I can proudly say I've done more than just live with it — I've truly lived! The beloved bicycle I had to sell when I was diagnosed (apparently riding was off the table) has been replaced by not one but a couple of shiny new bikes through the years.

I've joined several century and double-century bike Gran fondos, tandem raced in a half Ironman, swam with whale sharks and manta rays (yes, they're as majestic as they sound), and even learned to surf — despite still being super wobbly in the water (well, honestly, to this day, I still can't swim or even float!). Who needs mastery when you have enthusiasm?

I've rock climbed, rappelled down a cliff Mission Impossible fashion (yes, headfirst—why not add a little thrill), abseiled down waterfalls like a scene from another action movie, free-jumped off bridges sans ropes or harnesses into rivers to white water raft it (take that, fear!), hang-glided over Brazilian rainforests like a bird on vacation, and even done backflips and executed a full short program on a real outdoor flying trapeze (till now I wonder how perpetually-dizzy-Me did that!). All those wild adventures I once thought my body couldn't handle? Consider them checked off my imaginary list!

I never got around to making a bucket list because it hit me: life isn't meant to be confined by lists—it's one grand adventure waiting to unfold! When new experiences come knocking at my door, I simply check in with my body and see how it feels that day. Life offers chances for a reason; if my condition allows me to seize them, then why not dive in headfirst?

Sure, I know there are things I may never get to do— and that's perfectly okay! Each day I wake up is a gift wrapped in possibilities. We all have our crosses to bear and hurdles that limit us, but we also have what it takes to get through them or accept those that we have to stay on the sidelines for & watch, admire & feel the gift of awe looking at somebody else do so.

As for that hole in my head)? Yep, it's still there! My latest CT scan confirmed what I already know: it's not getting better anytime soon unless I opt for surgery. And while I'm still contemplating whether or not to go under the knife (who doesn't love a good craniotomy?), I've embraced what I call the Non-Bucket-List Life. No checklists or expectations—just wide-open eyes ready for whatever life throws my way.

If that means chugging apple cider vinegar, moringa juice, turmeric tea, and all sorts of organic elixirs (even my daughter's extra breast milk!) while doing yoga, dry brushing, acupuncture, and other alternative therapies (which I actually enjoy), then bring it on! Nothing comes easy in this adventure called life.

And when those days come when my body or circumstances decide to take a "vacation", well, I've already missed out on three half Ironman relay events three years in a row because I was just too sick to get up — I've learned to just chalk it up to "timing sucks." After all, with all the incredible things I've done already, who am I to complain?

It's been almost three decades of living with my body's quirks, but looking back at how far I've come makes me realize that what once felt like a prison has actually set me free! Being "sick" isn't a death sentence; instead, it has liberated me and made me grateful for everything I have—my abilities and the people who love me—that's what truly matters.

Sick days are easier now; heartaches still sting but carry hopeful promises of healing. I've learned to listen to my imperfect body, embrace my limitations, and appreciate the beauty in what I have rather than lament what I don't.

For those of us facing challenges, we'll have good days and bad. But we can strive for more good days and learn to let go of the bad ones — or accept when we need to sit it out for a bit.

Don't let your limitations define you; life is one big mystery waiting to be explored as an adventure and no bucket list will ever help you do that!

The Non-Bucket List Life

In the quiet shadows where
dreams used to dwell,
I once chased the horizon with a story to tell.
With a bucket list clutched
like a lifeline in hand,
I raced toward the finish, but
life had other plans.

Milestones slipped by like
whispers in the night,
Each one a reminder of battles I'd fight.
Yet, in the stillness, I found a new way,
To cherish each heartbeat, to live day by day.

The Non-Bucket List Life
became my refrain,
A tapestry woven from joy and from pain.
With every small victory, I
learned to embrace,
The beauty of living, grateful for
blessings—no longer chased.

Chapter 4

In the garden of motherhood, joy
blooms with weeds of worry; each
flower embodies immeasurable love,
while every weed bears the weight of
helplessness as I watch my child wage a
battle I cannot fight for her.

Just when I finally began to wrap my mind around my own challenges and learned to manage my medical condition, life decided to pull the rug out from under me once again. My then twelve-year-old firstborn casually mentioned that she had been struggling with the stairs at school, sometimes feeling her legs freeze mid-step, leading to small tumbles. Thank goodness there were no major accidents—yet.

As any concerned mother would, my worry kicked in. After a heart-to-heart, I discovered that her hands also sometimes froze, curling into tight fists, needing a gentle nudge from her other hand to release them.

After navigating a maze of doctors, tests, and my hapless research on Mr. World Wide Web, my darling was diagnosed with Muscular Dystrophy.

My heart plummeted, and I was swept into a whirlpool of torment even more agonizing than my own diagnosis. Because this time, it wasn't me carrying the burden; it's my daughter. And no matter how fervently I wish the heavens would let me shoulder her pain, I know that's simply not how this works.

For some reason, right after the diagnosis was made, my daughter's condition developed a personality of its own, sprouting legs and dancing off into the sunset—like a diva demanding the spotlight, showcasing its most dreadful talents while auditioning for a role in a tragicomedy. Was it mere coincidence, or was the universe playing an especially twisted prank on me? Whatever the case, one thing was painfully clear: things were about to spiral into chaos and nosedive into the abyss, leaving me holding the popcorn and bracing for the next act of this absurd play.

And here's the harsh reality: there's no cure for this relentless foe. It feels like I'm caught in an unending battle, where each day brings fresh challenges and uncertainties, leaving me to navigate a landscape filled with both hope and heartache.

It's a lot to take in, I know. But I'm grateful we have a name for what we're up against, and I have hope in our corner. With a lot of love, we will face this challenge head-on, one day at a time. My girl is a fighter, and I'm not going anywhere. We've got this!

But I must admit, grappling with this new reality has been a wild and turbulent ride. The first year, as we struggled to comprehend the full weight of this disease and its impact on my beloved Yssa, left me gasping for air. Anxiety became her shadow, with her muscles seizing up at the most inconvenient moments, transforming everyday life into a series of unexpected skirmishes.

At first, it was just her fists clenching tightly and the occasional knee buckling. But as time marched on, the condition crept forward, evolving into something far more menacing than we ever anticipated.

Countless times, I would receive frantic calls from her, her voice trembling as she described the agony of her entire arm caught in an unrelenting grip of muscle flexing. It hurt so much that she felt overwhelmed by the pain. As time went on, this torment spread like wildfire, creeping down from her knee to her toes and then advancing even further, engulfing her whole leg in its merciless grasp.

You know that feeling at the gym when you lift weights and see your muscles harden as you flex them? It takes effort and control, right? For her, it was as if her muscles had become rebellious teenagers—flexing on their own, eager to show off without any invitation. The tension would be frozen in place like a copy-pasted image on your laptop, refusing to budge. It became excruciating for her, as those muscles wouldn't relax, turning what should have been a moment of strength into a relentless cycle of pain.

Every single time she called, I would spring into action, no matter where I was—whether I was in the middle of my toilet time, stuck in a meeting, or wrestling with a grocery cart. I joked that I could apply to be an ambulance driver, having mastered the fine art of weaving through city traffic at breakneck speed.

I would rush to her side and massage those rebellious muscles. With gentle hands and soothing words, I'd tell her she'll be alright, slowly working to straighten them out. At first, it would take five minutes; then, it stretched to ten. But as the condition advanced, those moments of relief could drag on for an hour or more.

And then there were those heart-wrenching episodes when her entire body would seize up—her arms locked in place, her torso rigid, even her neck caught in this cruel grip. It felt as if she had transformed into a statue of anguish, and all I could do was stand by, hoping to breathe life back into her frozen form.

Oh, I can't begin to describe the excruciating agony it brought to her, me, and our family to witness her in that state for what felt like an eternity—minutes stretching into hours. Each time, it was as if a piece of me crumbled away, leaving me feeling hollow and helpless, watching my child endure this torment day in and day out, multiple times a day. It was like being trapped in a never-ending horror movie, where the suspense never lifted, and the only way to find relief was to hit the pause button—if only for a fleeting moment. If only I could...

On one particularly gloomy day, I received that dreaded call from her school: she was having one of her episodes. My heart raced as I sped down the road, a whirlwind of anxiety and determination swirling within me, ready to swoop in and save her once again. When I finally arrived in the mid-afternoon light, I found the classroom empty; her classmates were told to go outside for an activity, leaving her alone in a world that felt too big and too cruel.

There she was, slumped in her chair, utterly frozen—unable to move even a finger. My heart sank, knowing she must have endured an embarrassing spectacle as her classmates watched her transfixed in that position. I could sense her anxiety pulsing through the air, a thick fog that only intensified with each passing moment, making it even harder for her muscles to find any semblance of relaxation.

I tried everything — the usual gentle words, soothing touches, but nothing worked. Her embarrassed anxiety was too strong against my efforts to relax her muscles. As we watched the sun dip below the horizon outside the window, painting the sky with hues of orange and purple and then black, it struck me: night had fallen while she remained trapped in that same agonizing pose for a few hours already. Exhaustion was etched on her face, but the awkward angle of her body made any chance of rest impossible.

With my heart breaking into a million jagged pieces, I carefully carried my child and laid her on the ground, hoping to give her some semblance of respite from this afternoon's ordeal. Feeling utterly powerless to free her from this frozen state, I dropped to my knees and lay down beside her. In that moment, I wanted to share her pain, to let her know she wasn't alone, even in this painfully uncomfortable position.

I can still vividly recall that dusty classroom floor as we lay there, facing each other. I wrapped my arms around her, feeling the weight of our shared struggle pressing down on us. The world outside continued its relentless march forward, but in that moment, time stood still for us, two souls intertwined in a battle against an unrelenting adversary. In that embrace, we both understood — our lives had forever changed.

Yssa's Riddle

In shadows and light, I gracefully sway,
A paradox wrapped in love's warm array.
I cradle the joy that can cut like a knife,
With a love so profound, it shapes all of life.

What am I, this bond that forever will last,
A journey of futures entwined with the past?

I hold both the joy and the deepest of pain,
In my tender embrace, both
sunshine and rain.
I nurture your dreams while
I carry the weight,
In my arms lies a love that can never abate.

What am I, this path of both
sorrow and mirth,
The greatest of gifts that
brings forth new birth?

I am the whisper in the stillness of night,
A blend of pure joy and unfathomable fright.
I cradle your hopes while I
mourn what may be,
A bond woven tightly, just you and me.

What am I? This journey
both heavy and sweet,
A blessing and burden where
heartbeats meet?

I am Motherhood, a Love complete...

Chapter 5

Hope whispers; hope persists...
it remains despite and resists our disbelief.
Hope lingers; hope endures ... it
stands resilient through what our faith
ensures.

Alright, folks, let's pause the dramatic symphony of heartache for a moment, shall we? Seriously, who decided we should be living off painful milestones like they're the only dish on the menu? Come on! It's time to sprinkle some joy into this recipe of life!

So, hold onto your socks; I promise this next bit will have "happy" written all over it—like a neon sign in a dark alley! Trust me, we're about to turn this emotional rollercoaster into a bit of a joyride, too.

Picking up from that emotional moment on the floor — yes, the one where I felt like I was auditioning for a role in a heart-wrenching drama; there's really only one way to go from rock bottom: up. When you've reached the depths of despair, the only choice left is to rise, even if it feels daunting.

After finally embracing the reality of our situation (and allowing myself a moment to grieve), I buckle up and prepare for what lies ahead. As always, research is my weapon of choice, my trusty sidekick - it gives me a sense of control in the chaos (because who needs superpowers when you have Google at your fingertips?). Toss in an occasional splash of whiskey on the weekends and a generous serving of 2,000 Hail Mary's for good measure, and I'm all set to face whatever madness comes my way.

But before we dive headfirst into this happily ever after, I must throw in a little reality check. We can't just skip over the tough stuff — because that's how life rolls in the real world. There's rarely a moment when everything is smooth sailing; the real trick is in how we choose to see those challenges, don't you think? It's all about finding the silver linings hidden in the storm clouds!

So, the reality was that my daughter's condition continued to worsen. We had to decide to leave our home and move to a three-bedroom condo in the middle of the city so we could be near the hospital for any emergency. Then, it reached a point where she could no longer walk. We found ourselves pushing her around on a computer chair with wheels, trying to prepare her for the idea of being wheelchair-bound.

We even started looking at motorized chairs, attempting to spark her excitement about driving her own ride around the mall. I told her just to imagine the envy on her sisters' faces! Anything to distract from the bitter truth that she might never walk again.

And as if that wasn't enough, one day she woke up and said, "Mom, I can't see!" At that moment, I felt my heart drop so hard I couldn't even find it on the floor so I could pick it back up. It was a gut-wrenching reminder of how fragile our already shattered dreams can be.

After a couple of weeks in the hospital (I practically lived there already), with a revolving door of doctors who couldn't figure out the cause of her sudden blindness, we finally caught a break from heaven. We found a doctor who cracked the case wide open. He put in a request for me to be present in the operating room during her surgery. She needed to be awake for it, and I was the only one who could keep her calm and talk her through the procedure so her muscles wouldn't do a bout of statue dance while she was on the operating table.

After signing all the waivers and enduring a thorough briefing that felt like preparing for a space mission, I took a deep breath and steeled myself with my best "everything will be okay" face. I wanted to show my daughter that despite the odds, we could face this together with unwavering faith; all the while, I was shaking uncontrollably inside from fright.

As I stood there, heart racing, I reminded myself that everything would be alright after this ordeal. It had to be. Please, God, let it be! This was our moment to reclaim hope, and I was determined to walk with her through it.

Fast forward from that fateful day, and despite the other hiccups we had to go through in this wild medical rollercoaster we've been riding —complete with unexpected twists and stomach-dropping turns that I won't subject you to anymore (consider it my gift to you) — I'm absolutely over the moon to say we've made it through, so far! My daughter regained her sight after the surgery, a moment that felt like hitting the jackpot in the lottery of hope. It was as if the universe decided to toss us a much-needed lifeline, reminding us that miracles can happen when you least expect them.

Then, in a stroke of luck that could only be described as divine intervention, I stumbled upon a magical massage bed with jade stones. This was the answer to my hopes for a better course of action, even if it wouldn't offer a permanent cure (certainly so much better than the powerless feeling of not being able to do anything) — one that didn't just mask her symptoms with a parade of medications that would've eventually destroyed her kidneys but actually offered real relief. Seriously, this thing could practically have its own "Do Not Disturb" sign for all the relaxation it provides, not to mention the incredible help it has been in calming her muscles down, which has greatly abated her episodes.

In what felt like an instant, all the worry and heartache faded into the background, replaced by a bright spark of possibility. She can walk again, and the wheelchair-bound life has been tucked away (for now...forever, I hope). We were back in the game, and I couldn't help but feel that maybe, just maybe, the best chapters of our story were still ahead!

Now, she indulges in two full rounds on that heavenly contraption every single day, and it's like watching her drift into a serene oasis. Each session feels like a mini-vacation from her struggles, and I can't help but marvel at how something so simple can bring such profound comfort.

This routine has worked wonders! While she still experiences episodes of frozen muscles a couple of times daily (I like to call them her "statue moments"), she no longer has those full-body episodes that feel like a scene from a horror movie. Instead, she's become a master at adapting, learning to relax and unfreeze her muscles like a pro yogi amid chaos.

Thank God for plot twists and unexpected breaks! We may not have achieved the bright future every mother dreams for her child, but we've at least regained hope.

Whatever the future holds, I believe it will bring not just sad stories but also joyful milestones along the way.

Heavenly cheers to that!!!

**Shadows and Light:
A Mother's Journey**

In the heart of motherhood, a paradox unfolds,
A love so profound, yet heavy as it holds.
A gift wrapped in burdens,
both tender and tough,
A wild ride of joy, yet the road can be rough.

With every heartbeat shared, a mother's soul entwines,
Bearing the weight of her child's hopes and signs.
In the depths of her being, she feels every ache,
Wishing to carry their pain for their own sake.

Through sleepless nights and tears that fall like rain,
She stands as a fortress against all the pain.
Each sorrow she shields them from, a silent vow,
To bear the burdens they face—oh, if only somehow.

Yet amid the shadows where grief often dwells,
There flickers a light that whispers and swells.
For even in darkness, hope starts to ignite,
A beacon of love that guides through the night.

Through every struggle and trial they face,
A source of unlimited divine love, a saving grace...
And though the path may twist through valleys so deep,
There's always a light at the end and hope to keep.

Chapter 6

Here's to the beginning of a new journey...
where love transforms, memories
linger, and strength is found in letting
go.

Alright, listen up because I'm about to drop some truth bombs here. I always knew the day would come when my little birdies would fly the coop and leave me to my own devices. I thought it would be like a casual goodbye — like, "See ya later, alligator!" Let's be real; they can't just hang around my house forever, living rent-free and raiding my snack stash, right? I did have a taste of the empty nester syndrome when my youngest started whole-day elementary school, and I was left all by myself all afternoon with nothing to do except count the hours till I had to pick them all up! That wasn't fun for me at all! I felt utterly useless! I almost lost it, to be honest! So,

I thought that was the worst of it! It's like getting chicken pox when you're young, which means you're not getting it a second time anymore! Wrong!!!! I knew it would be a big deal of a milestone, sure! But did I think it would REALLY be a big deal when they finally spread their wings? Heck, no! I was ready to do the happy dance and reclaim my throne as the remote-control queen!

So, yeah, I thought it would be a breeze. Look, I've raised 3 teenage girls —how hard can this be? So, at that point, I self-talked myself and had my 'If you'll excuse me, I'm off to plan my next adventure' speech ready. Maybe I'll take up skydiving (if they'd let me) or learn how to speak dog language and be the next dog whisperer. Anything to fill the void left by my little hatchlings. Although I must admit, it is kind of nice to have the remote all to myself again. Silver linings folks!

But life loves to remind me on a daily basis that my grasp on this universe is about as solid as a marshmallow in a campfire. Yep! Life just keeps shoving it in my face, like a big ol' pie made of "I told you so" and "Surprise, you're human!"

So here I am, trying to navigate this whole empty nest situation, and it's like my emotions are having a dance party in my head. One minute I'm doing the "Hallelujah,

I'm free!" jig, and the next, I'm ugly-crying to the "My Babies Are Grown Up" Waltz. It's a real mess, let me tell you.

Oh, and did I mention that my kids just up and decided to attend university a gazillion miles away? That's right, they packed their dreams and headed to Midland, Michigan—because who wouldn't want to trade the sun-kissed beaches and tropical paradise of the Philippines for the icy embrace of the Midwest, the land of snow and… well, more snow? It's like they're on a mission to see just how much they can make me sweat (in the land of snow and…well, more snow!)

Here's the deal: It's a solid two to three days by air and land travel just to reach them if I feel the urgent need to check in — like a superhero mom on a mission armed with snacks and a first-aid kit! Honestly, I think they're just enjoying the thrill of watching me juggle my anxiety while they sip hot cocoa in their cozy dorm rooms.

Picture this: there I am, a little Asian woman fueled by caffeine and sheer determination, navigating airports like I'm in an extreme sport! I'll be hopping into a rental car to drive to the next city, wrestling with my oversized suitcase — stuffed to the brim with Purefoods corned beef and enough Pancit Canton instant noodles to feed a small city. Seriously, you'd think I was packing for an apocalypse! Apparently, these treasures can't be found in their local stores (and to be honest, if mom's bringing it in, it's free), so it's up to me to deliver the goods.

Cheers to higher education and my new role as a professional worrywart and grocery delivery service! Who knew my biggest adventure would involve dodging security lines and ensuring my kids don't starve in the land of frozen pizza and burgers?

And after flying into the land of snow and more snow (Wait, did I already say that?... I just can't get over how much snow there is there!) to get them settled, stocking their fridge and dorm pantry with the essentials—rice, cup noodles, and Spam, the Pinoy version holy trinity of college survival, I make the same two-three day trip back to an empty home. The moment I step through the door, it hits me: the silence is deafening. It's like walking into a museum dedicated to my former life as a hands-on mom.

When that day finally arrived, it was like someone flipped a switch. Major Milestone Alert!!! Suddenly, my home went from a bustling family hub to a ghost town faster than you can say "empty nester." I was ready to break out the confetti and celebrate my newfound freedom! But instead, I found myself staring at the walls like they were long-lost friends. Who knew silence could feel so loud?

I find myself reaching for the phone, about to call them, before remembering they're off on their own adventure now — probably debating whether instant ramen counts as a food group. My little birds have flown the nest, and I'm left with just the memories of their smiles, the echoes of their voices, and an overwhelming sense of nostalgia. I mean, who knew that stocking up on Spam would become my love language? It's a bittersweet feeling, like a gentle tug on my heartstrings.

But deep down, I know this is what I raised them for — to spread their wings in a world full of possibilities. And as much as I miss them, I know this is how it's supposed to be. So I straightened my shoulders, wiped away a stray tear (ok, fine, I bawled my eyes out first), and reminded myself that I raised them to be strong, independent women, ready to take on the world.

So I take a deep breath, embrace the quiet, and remind myself that this is just part of the journey.

The Empty Nester's Cheer

Hip, hip, hooray, we're finally free!
Like kids let out for recess, dancing with glee.
No more carpool chaos or late-night stress,
Feels like living our dreams, I must confess.

But hold up a minute, what's this I feel?
A twinge of loneliness that's all too real!
Where'd all the laughter and wild antics go?
Just me and my thoughts on
a one-woman show!

Now it doesn't feel right to
shout hip hip hooray,
Can't decide if I want them to go or to stay.
This isn't turning out as fun as
I thought it would be,
But we're here, so let's embrace
this chapter, then wait and see.

Chapter 7

Midlife Crisis: The Unquiet Awakening.
This is not a collapse—it's a resurrection!
A mission to reclaim your identity, to
rewrite the script of your soul, to burn
the masks that suffocated you and rise
from the ashes of what you thought you
were.

To be perfectly honest, I didn't think I'd go through a midlife crisis. Yeah, right! I was one of those people, too — Denial was my middle name! Looking back, I started mourning my youth way too early. The moment I hit 30, it felt like an alarm went off: "Crisis time!" (Apparently, at that age, it was premature!) Maybe I was aging in dog years, and my body thought it had already hit midlife while everyone else was still busy figuring out how to adult without Googling everything!

I chalked it up to cramming at least two decades' worth of drama into my twenties—seriously! Between battling depression, juggling my health issues, and managing the physical and financial weight of three kids along with a mountain of medical bills, it felt like I was living a lifetime's worth of chaos in just one decade.

My twenties flew by while I was busy cranking out babies and transforming them into toddlers. Now, those little whirlwinds have happily ditched me for school all day long, mimicking preterm empty nesting! By the time I hit thirty, it felt like my life had already fast-forwarded through the angst of a midlife crisis, complete with plot twists, triumphs, and enough epic facepalms to fill a blooper reel! It's as if I blinked and suddenly landed in the "Where Did My Youth Go?" Club, complete with an endless supply of mom jeans and a collection of half-finished novels.

The upside to this premature onset was that during my thirties, I was mostly wobbly, dizzy, and glued to my bed, thanks to my then-undiagnosed condition; my daughter was just starting to notice her own set of symptoms, too, so we were drowning in a whirlwind of drama that felt like a never-ending telenovela. Honestly, I couldn't tell if all the tears and emotional upheavals were from my midlife crisis or just the universe throwing us one curveball after another! My hands were so full that my brain didn't even have time to analyze or overanalyze my midlife journey. Thank goodness for that — who needs self-reflection when you're busy navigating the chaotic maze of existence?

And so, by the time I finally emerged from that tumultuous decade, feeling like I had outmaneuvered that "crisis," I threw open the doors to my forties with a fresh perspective that was still wide open to whatever life decided to hurl at me. Armed with a treasure trove of hard-earned wisdom and a hefty share of drama, I transformed "Que sera, sera" into my battle cry, ready to tackle anything worth stressing about, declaring to the universe, "Bring it on! I've got this!"

So here's my first brilliant idea for how a middle-aged mom of three spends her newly found extra time: (drum roll, please) learning to ride on a Harley Davidson bike! Because nothing screams, "I've got my life together," like zooming down the highway on a roaring motorcycle with the wind in my hair and a questionable grasp on the rules of the road.

Who needs yoga when I can unleash my inner rebel and feel like a rockstar, completely decked out in a biker chic jacket and boots? Watch out, world—this mom is trading in her family car for a big bike!

Let me share the comedic highlights of my grand entrance into the world of riding the big guns! Picture this: here I am, standing at a towering 5 feet 2 inches and weighing in at a solid 125 pounds, thinking I could handle a motorcycle that weighed nearly five times my body weight. Spoiler alert: I was hilariously mistaken!

In a moment of sheer audacity, I wrangled my husband into handing down his Harley Street to me when he bought a new bike. With all the bravado of a seasoned biker (shame on me), I declared that he'd never have to back-ride me again because I would be one of the few women in our city riding solo! What a show-off! What was I thinking?

As I approached that beast, I felt like a Chihuahua challenging a Great Dane—adorably optimistic but utterly outmatched. When I finally swung my leg over the seat, my legs were so short they practically waved goodbye to the ground! I looked like a toddler on a grown-up's bike, teetering precariously and wondering if I'd need training wheels just to stay upright.

But hey, common sense is overrated when you have determination! So, off I went on a quest worthy of an epic adventure: hunting for super platform riding boots that would give me just enough height to reach the ground without looking like I was auditioning for "Biker Babies." After scouring every mall and diving deep into the depths of the internet, I finally found my golden ticket — the perfect pair of boots that would elevate me from "adorably challenged" to "ready to ride!". Now, with my new boots and an unwavering spirit, I was ready to conquer the open road, just as soon as I figured out how to start the motorcycle without accidentally launching myself into orbit!

Let me set the scene: poor hubby was roped into being my designated instructor — bless his heart! I was way too self-conscious to sign up for a class. And I was too busy (frankly embarrassed too) basking in my own overconfidence to admit that learning to ride a big bike, especially a Harley (which everyone claimed was one of the toughest to master), might be a tad ambitious.

You have to understand that I was an utter newbie. The concept of gears and shifting on a motorcycle was as alien to me as trying to decipher hieroglyphics! With my tiny hands—barely bigger than a toddler's—it felt like I was trying to grip a giant banana while attempting to hold up a bike at an uphill stoplight. Let me tell you, that was almost torture! The first ride alone gave me carpal tunnel!

But I was determined, so I sucked it up and pressed on. I mean, come on! I thought figuring out steps 1 to 20 of riding that beast was a bit of a puzzle, but I'm no stranger to a good brain teaser! Ehhhhh, wrong! So there I was, with my husband trying to teach me the intricacies of motorcycle riding while I wondered if I could somehow will the bike to obey me with sheer brainpower. Surprise! It did not work!

Time to pivot to Plan B! The long and winding, old-fashioned road of practice! That's right—every day (well, let's say 3-5 times a week), we'd head over to our neighborhood cemetery. I know, I know—it sounds a bit morbid, but trust me, if you're from our neck of the woods, it makes perfect sense! There I was, zipping around amidst the gravestones like a scene from a quirky horror movie, channeling my inner ghost rider. After all that practice and a lot of graveyard grit, I finally got the hang of it! Yessss!!! Milestone earned!!!

So you'd think that's the end of my saga, right? Wrong! When I finally emerged from the tranquil roads of the memorial park, I quickly realized that all I could do was ride straight down the road and, at best, make right turns! ONLY right turns!!!

I don't know what spirit I needed to exorcise, but left turns were like some kind of mystical curse. U-turns? Forget it! I was basically a one-way street on two wheels!

For a couple of weeks, I was on a relentless quest—turning left was like trying to solve a Rubik's Cube blindfolded! My husband and I became dizzy strategists, mapping out routes that allowed me to only make right turns. It felt like we were training for the "Tour de Right" just to get to the grocery store and back!

Can you imagine? We spun around like a broken record, with our GPS stuck on 'recalculating'. Honestly, I'm amazed we didn't go completely crazy trying to stick to those right-turn routes! To this day, we can't help but laugh until our sides hurt whenever we reminisce about my epic showdown with left turns.

We'd been at this for a solid two or three weeks, and it hit me: I wasn't making any progress at all! Every ride felt like I was hitting the reset button, starting from square one. At this rate, I'd never learn to ride!

So, in a moment of desperation, I pulled out my secret weapon for these kinds of things—my second daughter, Yanna, who was now a million miles away. She's my designated "baby boy," the closest thing I have to one, even though she's the ultimate girly girl, too. Somehow, she has this magical ability to hypnotize me into tackling the challenging stuff I set out to do. Plus, she's like my ever-vigilant security guard, always making sure I'm okay!

I dialed her up and blurted out, "Help! I don't know if I'll ever get the hang of this!" She knows how much I loathe falling short of my ambitious and sometimes downright crazy goals. Plus, I've already asked for this bike I might not really be able to use!

Then she hit me with her classic coach tone—the one that could motivate a sloth to run a marathon—and said, "Mom, just order some cute riding outfits (she knows me too well) and hop on that bike! Don't think—just go!"

And just like that, I felt a spark of determination. Who knew all it took was a little fashion advice and some tough love from my daughter to get me back in the saddle? After that, the rest was biker chick history!

Midlife Crisis: A Recipe

Ingredients:

1 cup of existential dread (freshly brewed in the void of your 40s)

½ cup of nostalgia (stale, but oddly comforting)

A pinch of "I'm too old for this" (sprinkle liberally over every TikTok trend)

Optional:

1 dash of "What's my purpose? (add to taste, or until you cry)

A Harley Davidson Big Bike (or a sports car—same energy)

Instructions:

1. Mix until chaotic.
2. Serve with a side of irony.
3. Garnish with a poem you'll never publish.

Chapter 8

We each bear our own mountains to climb...
the peaks that pierce the sky,
the valleys that carve the soul.
Through these journeys, we earn the
right to stand at the summit, to raise
our hands to the heavens, and to roar—
'I have truly lived!'

At this point, I'm embracing my 47-year-old Biker Chic persona, pinching myself and doing double-takes in the mirror, wondering, "Is that really me?" I've even snagged an officer seat in the Harley Owners Group! Now I'm rolling with the big guys, feeling like a rockstar on wheels. Who would've thought I had it in me? Not this gal! Cue the happy dance and air guitar, will ya!

But with my attention-deficit mind that zooms faster than my bike on a sugar rush, it's only a matter of time before I hatch another wildly outrageous idea — much to the eye-rolling exasperation of my husband and mother.

In just a few "rediscovery" years, I've morphed into a challenge crusader! Is this my real midlife crisis? By now, I've tackled the Giro de Luca, a grueling three-day bicycle race (200 km on Day 1, 155 on Day 2, and 144 km on Day 3 — also coaching my youngest daughter to join me on the final day). I've rock climbed the Batu Caves in Kuala Lumpur, summited Snow Mountain in Taiwan, Mount Fuji in Japan, and Mount Toubkal in Morocco; all while my mind fired off ideas like fireworks on New Year's Eve!

One day, in a fit of spontaneous brilliance (or madness), I declared, "I'm climbing Mt. Everest Base Camp!". Cue the dramatic music and my mom's horrified expression—she looked like I had just announced I was joining a circus or adopting a pet alligator. But, when life hands you mountains, you strap on your boots and climb them, right?!

After the thrill of my grand declaration faded, reality splashed me like a bucket of ice water: I might have just signed up for mission impossible! First off, I completely forgot about the hole in my head that's sensitive to cerebral pressure changes. Even a little strain during a bout of constipation or a heavy-ish cry-sesh during a sappy movie turns my head into a sold-out concert — loud, chaotic, and triggering all my symptoms like a rockstar with a mic!

I wondered how on earth high altitude and a lack of oxygen at 17,000 feet would treat me. Oops! Looks like I might have jumped the gun ... again! Seriously, what was I thinking? But hey, who needs common sense when you dream of conquering Everest?

The first thing I had to do was prove to my husband that I was fit enough for the extreme 12-day trek so he would sign off on it. First stop: my Neuro Otologist. When I asked her for medical clearance, her reaction was priceless: "Why don't you just do a helicopter tour? I did that, too! It's much easier and safer! Clearly, she doesn't know me very well—or my penchant for self-inflicted torture!

But seeing my determination to "embrace my inner adventure junkie," and after I swore on a stack of protein bars that I would listen to my body and take care of myself, she took a deep breath and transformed into a medical detective. With the intensity of a surgeon about to perform brain surgery, she began her thorough check.

She peered into my ears like she was searching for buried treasure, twisted my head this way and that as if trying to unlock a secret code, and had me focus on her nose while she spun me around like a carnival ride operator.

After what felt like an Olympic-level examination, she finally declared, "Well, you're surprisingly healthy! I guess you can go on your little escapade."

Alrighty, I'm all set! But where on earth do I even begin? I had no clue and didn't know anyone who'd done it before. So, I turned to my biking buddies, thinking they'd be my trusty sidekicks. Instead, they erupted into laughter like I'd suggested riding our bikes to the moon!

Then my mini-me (my youngest daughter, Tia) caught wind of my plans and practically catapulted out of her chair like a caffeinated kangaroo! Apparently, this was on her wish list, too! I realized I'd rubbed off on her and all three kids—how could I say no? With more tattoos than the rest of the family combined, I'm basically the ambassador of crazy ideas. So here we are, three months away from E Day, diving headfirst into this madness together! What could possibly go wrong? Ummm, a lot!

We started with the basics: breaking-in our trek shoes while getting our walking muscles and lungs in fighting shape. Living on the 32nd floor turned our daily workout into an epic stair-climbing saga. We strutted up and down all 32 floors — talk about a cardio adventure!

For added oomph, we opted for the fire escape stairs — no windows, zero ventilation and sometimes we would even wear altitude training masks! Who needs fresh air when you can do high-altitude training in a claustrophobic metal box? It's a completely made-up training strategy, but, why not?

Some days, we'd venture outdoors, hauling ourselves up the hilliest city roads with jeepneys and motorcycles, loading backpacks with gear to mimic trek weight — sweating buckets while pretending to be mountain climbers! Picture us trudging like overzealous pack mules, gasping for breath, looking like we were auditioning for "Extreme Hiking: The Struggle is Real!"

During one of our outdoor training treks, disaster struck! My daughter's knee suddenly and very painfully gave out, forcing her to be picked up while I trudged home alone for three more hours— talk about a dramatic exit!

Her old triathlon injury had resurfaced, and after an MRI and doctor visits, it was clear she wouldn't heal in time for our trek. I tried to stay positive, but just thinking we wouldn't share this milestone and create unforgettable memories together was crushing. My confidence plummeted as I faced the challenge alone as the only awkward wannabe mountaineer in the group with just two months of training and a resume of failed attempts!

I was lucky to have two friends from Hong Kong joining me, but they were seasoned trekkers with more experience than mountain goats! I could already picture them effortlessly scaling cliffs while I struggled to keep up, panting like a dog in a sauna. I had to suck it up and keep training — if I didn't want to end up at the foot of the mountain, regretting my big mouth!

So, I soldier on with my biweekly fire escape climbs and weekend warrior treks, flying solo. A month before the day, my old biking knee injury decided to join the party, feeling left out, I guess! I had to toss out that last precious month for cram-training to do the mandatory rest for my injury to recoup like I wasn't about to do a death walk to Base Camp soon!

Fast-forward through the drama: I land in Kathmandu at midnight, fashionably late and a few training weeks short to give my knee time to heal.

I'm the last of our twelve-person Philippine team to arrive, missing all introductions. My roommate, whom I've never met (who was supposed to be my daughter), is already appropriately snoozing like a hibernating bear in our room, ready to start our 12-day trek the next day. Another day in my life… where everything's the harder, Game B sleep-deprived version!

The first day was a whirlwind of excitement and jitters. The flight to Lukla was an adventure in itself; I fought for the front-row seat behind the pilot; front-row view of the world's wildest roller coaster!

As we soared through the skies, I clung to my seat like a toddler on a sugar high, marveling at the breathtaking views approaching the most dangerous airport in the world. Landing at Lukla felt like an action movie scene, with the runway perched on a cliff and a drop that could make anyone's stomach do backflips. Just another day in paradise!

This is it! I won't bore you with a blow-by-blow, just a quick run-through of highlights because retelling would leave me panting, just like during the trek! Each day was a reality show mix of sweat, tears, and existential crises.

I can still picture that first hour navigating boulders. Nothing death-defying, but thank heavens my daughter wasn't with me; her knees would have staged a full protest, complete with picket signs and dramatic speeches! That reminded me that there's always a reason for everything— even disappointments. Sometimes, you just have to let go of failed attempts to spot that elusive rainbow, probably lounging on the other side with a piña colada, chuckling at our antics!

The third day took us to 3,600 meters, where I saw the "Peak of Heaven." By then, my backpack was growing roots on my back; my aging shoulders were in constant revolt; my swollen knees were throwing a tantrum, and I was missing my family terribly, but my first glimpse of Everest made all that momentarily go away. The mountain seemed to say, "Welcome to the party! Now stop whining and enjoy the view!"

After that, we were told to skip baths altogether or risk losing all our energy. As Little Ms. Tropics, perpetually drenched in sweat back home, the thought of it getting even colder was mind-boggling — yet it did!

Imagine me battling the elements like a tropical fish out of water, longing for a hot shower while my body was busy shivering and negotiating with my sanity. At least I can say I've mastered the art of staying dirty in style!

I remember splurging on hot water for my flask (because in the mountain, that spelled big bucks), which I affectionately dubbed my "sleeping bag buddy." I clung to it like a lifeline in my sleeping bag, along with my socks and the next day's clothes; otherwise, those would've turned to ice if I left it out. Who knew a flask could be both a source of warmth and a fashion statement in the freezing wilderness?

Oh, the things I learned in those days! Each challenge was a lesson wrapped in frostbite and sweat. How is it possible to shake from cold while sweating? It's like my body suddenly went bi-polar!

I got to know myself better, too. I discovered that I could endure more than I ever imagined. Oh wait, I already learned that with childbirth — all three times!!! So, I guess a better way to put it is that I was reminded of lessons I had already learned and got to appreciate the milestone of seeing just how far I've grown.

That was the mindset that kept me calm and collected during one of our typical lunches of rice and noodles when I suddenly had a fierce bout of Gerd— or whatever that was. My throat just closed up, and all the food felt stuck. I could barely breathe!

In that moment of panic, all I could think about was how to silently puke it out to clear my airway without anyone noticing my struggle. I was genuinely worried I'd make a scene and that they'd have to hail a helicopter to rescue me, all while I'd be left unable to finish the trek! Do you see how my mind becomes a crazy blade when I'm in this trance? — razor focus sharpened by obsession, cutting through reason, slicing time, until all that remains is the target… and the cost of reaching it.

Can you imagine trying to maintain your cool while rummaging through my pack for a plastic bag to catch my vomit, ever so graciously banging my stomach on the side of the table in my version of the Heimlich maneuver, all while my body was on the verge of convulsing for air? All that and still trying to look like I was just sitting there, casually chewing my food like it was a lovely Sunday brunch and not actually choking on it!

To this day, I shake my head at that one. I couldn't decide if it was a ridiculously stupid feat or determination at its finest. Let's just call it a tie and say it was the stupidest show of brave determination ever! Hooray for my utter stubbornness, aka stupidity in disguise!!!

That "feat" (if we can even call it that) sucked the last drop of energy from my altitude-challenged body halfway thru the trek. Opening my Kitkat bar felt like bench-pressing a mountain while simultaneously trying to play jazz trumpet underwater — breathtaking … literally!

From then on, I just got weaker. My body declared full-scale war. Every cell staged a protest against this high-altitude invasion. Lunch stops became narcolepsy festivals. I'd sit down, backpack still attached, and instantly transform into a sitting-up Sleeping Beauty. I just couldn't keep my eyes open! My appetite? Completely AWOL. Those once-tempting fried rice and noodles now looked like punishment. My survival kit? Colostrum powder and Rosquillos cookies—my holy grail of mountain nutrition. And the bathroom runs? Let's just say the mountain became my very inconvenient, very public restroom.

On my worst day, I asked my two friends to sandwich me in my sleeping bag between them. I was worried I might not wake up the next day I wanted them to hear me breathing!

There I was, cocooned like a burrito, while my friends probably questioned their life choices. "Just in case," I said, trying to sound casual. At least if I snored loudly enough, they'd know I was still alive—though they might have wished otherwise by morning!

During the trek, I often found myself running on empty, wondering if the next helicopter rescue would be my grand exit. But somehow, my stubbornness outweighed my common sense (and my backpack).

At the start of a particular day, we noticed a black crow hovering over us. Someone joked it was bad luck, and we laughed it off— until the mountain proved them right. What are the chances that of all days that was THE day altitude sickness slammed hard on one of our younger teammates, he could hardly walk and it was too late in the day to call for rescue, in case it got down to it. The guides had no choice but to split up the group, sending some ahead to reach the next camp safely before dark as the weather suddenly turned bad.

That was the moment I felt the weight of the risk I had taken to be here. And still, I didn't second-guess my choice. Was I being reckless? They say age brings wisdom, but here, at the edge of the world, I'm not nearing 50. I'm just a stubborn soul who refuses to back down.

The final push to Base Camp was a war cry against the body I'd been saddled with since birth — a factory-defect model that's spent more nights in hospitals since childbirth than a frequent flyer in first class. But I'd long stopped being a patient. In college, I'd declared myself CEO of my own health, weaponizing defiance like a telemarketer on a mission. Yet on that day — the coldest, most unforgiving stretch of the trek, my childhood ghosts came roaring back; my old battles had returned with a vengeance. At that altitude, where oxygen levels were just half of what I'd known at sea level, every breath was a struggle. For someone who'd lived their life in the oxygen-rich shallows, every breath felt like drowning in a desert. My lungs burned with the thinness of the air, each inhale feeling like trying to drink from an empty cup. The mountain didn't care about my past victories or how far I'd come — it demanded more.

But here's the thing: I'd spent decades learning to breathe through brokenness. I'm not about to give up now! I knew one thing for sure: this body may be flawed, but it's mine, and it's carried me this far. So I kept going, step by grueling step, because quitting, for me, is never an option.

And then finally, we reached the end of this trek's painful, beautiful climb. My friend doubled over, retching into the snow, catching her vomit in a plastic bag. I was too weak to even puke out my exhaustion but with the meager strength I could muster I forced her to join me in a selfie of this big milestone we had just crossed together. We needed proof we weren't hallucinating this! Never mind the thought that the hiking day was not over as we had to head back to the previous night's camp to spend the night there. A few minutes to celebrate after, we turned and sprinted, the mountain's shadow chasing us like a predator. A few hours left to reach camp; a few hours to outrun the pending darkness that came with the setting sun... which meant, it was about to get really cold and what I wouldn't give just to be back in my sleeping bag. But all that didn't seem so daunting anymore, because we got what we came for, at last!

Those 12 days are both a blur and a 4K movie in my head now ... my brain's way of having its own identity crisis, much like my body during the trek. It's as if my memories are playing a game of hide-and-seek, with some moments crystal clear and others hiding behind a fog of exhaustion and altitude sickness.

This journey transformed me in ways words can barely touch. I arrived as a doubting "mid-lifing" traveler. I left as something more — a woman who discovered her own unexpected resilience high above the clouds where dreams and determination dance together.

So, I'll close this chapter with a whispered "Namaste" to the mountain's sacred spirits. Their silent courage echoed in every step I took, reminding me that true strength isn't about perfection but about showing up—flawed, breathless, but unyielding.

Who knew a tropical girl could find her warrior spirit in the most unexpected place? Certainly not me— and that's its own beautiful, messy magic.

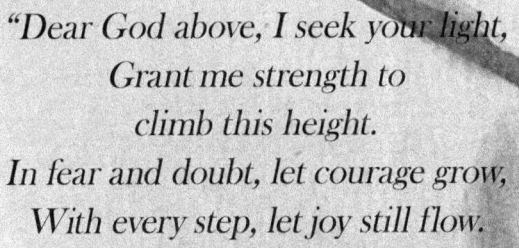

"Dear God above, I seek your light,
Grant me strength to
climb this height.
In fear and doubt, let courage grow,
With every step, let joy still flow.

Guide my heart and clear my way,
Help me shine through night and day.
In this challenge, let me see,
Your love and grace are guiding me."

Chapter 9

Breathe in, breathe out; Inhale peace, exhale
fear ... the rhythm of life's unspoken prayer.
Trust the journey, even when the path
bends into darkness. For in the end,
all will be fine — not because the storm
subsides, but because you've learned to
sway to the downpour's symphony.

See, the thing about milestones is that they are like those quirky roadside attractions on a road trip — they're not just one-and-done moments. You can't simply celebrate one and call it a day! They're life's markers and photo ops, the moments you pause for, snap a selfie, and say, "Wow, I did that!" You commit them to memory and then move on.

But as we've all figured out by now, not every milestone springs from happy moments or cinematic triumphs with a perfect ending. Some milestones emerge from the sad and fear-filled circumstances that life throws our way. They remind us that growth often comes from the toughest challenges, and sometimes, those very moments shape us the most.

So when the great COVID-19 pandemic rolled in, you can bet I had a story brewing! We all have our lockdown stories, but ours? It's a tale to tell.

There we were, perched on the 32nd floor like modern-day Rapunzels, our hair growing wild and our social skills withering. I became a master of the indoor marathon, expertly navigating from the bedroom to the living room. We practically operated an indoor gym, alternating between jump rope sessions, yoga, spin workouts, and high-intensity interval training.

But here's the thing—we weren't just surviving—we were creating our own bizarre, beautiful universe! We transformed our 120-square-meter world into a production studio that would make Hollywood directors look amateur. One day, we'd be shooting our own MTV-style music videos, choreographing songs and dance numbers where everyone was simultaneously the lead, backup dancer, make-up artist, cinematographer, and sound engineer; the next, we would be recording vlogs in the kitchen as if we knew what we were doing.

Scan these fo
proof of my
bragging righ

Our culinary adventures became legendary. Breakfast? More like an all-day affair! Arroz Caldo Sundays, Sisig Wednesdays, Spam Musubi Fridays— we assigned weekly meal themes like we were running a gourmet-restaurant-meets-family therapy session. Each dish was a rebellion against monotony, each meal a celebration of our creativity.

We weren't just passing time; we were crafting memories, constructing joy from the raw materials of lockdown. Our home became a stage, a kitchen, a dance floor, a beauty parlor, and most importantly, our sanctuary.

I literally did not step out of our door! My one daring adventure? A heart-pounding trip to the ground floor pharmacy and grocery. But then, oh, glorious day! I discovered the magic of door-to-door delivery and became one with my couch.

Time passed. The outside world became a distant memory, like wearing real pants or remembering what day it was. Then, plot twist! My architect husband ventured out for a site visit. One trip. One! And wouldn't you know it, he came back with an unwanted souvenir - COVID-19!

And here's the kicker - vaccines back then were as elusive as toilet paper in March 2020. This was a time when everything was hit or miss, and everyone was still grappling with how to fight this enormous enemy. Hospitals were packed, and lines for rooms were long, and first-generation Sinovac had just come out, and by this time, only doctors had been given a shot. We were left to face this invisible enemy armed with nothing but hand sanitizer and our wits.

When Dave's first sniffle echoed through our home, my worry bells didn't just ding—they erupted into a full-blown symphony of anxiety. With immune-compromised family members under our roof, this wasn't just a cold but a potential catastrophe waiting to unfold.

The moment that the home test kit flashed positive, I transformed into a one-woman emergency response team.

I packed Dave's bag like I was preparing for an apocalyptic getaway, booked a drive-thru COVID test faster than you can say "pandemic," and dispatched him to our beach house as if it were the last chopper out of a disaster zone.

Back at home base, I morphed into a whirlwind of disinfectant, UV lights, and instructions. I sanitized our bedroom with the fervor of a mad scientist, turning every surface into a germ-free wasteland. The kids received a crash course in "Pandemic Survival 101," complete with a strict "no touching anything Dad touched" policy.

With the condo transformed into a quarantine fortress, I raced to join Dave at our isolation station. Once a haven of relaxation, our beach house had become our personal COVID ward. There, I set up camp in the other bedroom, ready to play nurse from a safe distance. It was like a bizarre game of "The Sims: Pandemic Edition," where the goal was to keep everyone alive and COVID-free.

For days, I took on the role of a makeshift nurse armed with a cell phone and an arsenal of vitamins. I orchestrated a symphony of good nutrition, lung exercises, and sleep positions that would make a yoga instructor proud. Our daily routine consisted of temperature checks, oxygen level monitoring, and me waving from afar like a castaway on a desert island.

But then, the oximeter readings started to dip, and my heart sank faster than those numbers. When it hit 96, I called an ambulance; the last thing I wanted was for him to attempt the hour-long drive to the hospital, even if I would be following him in another car.

The ER became my new stage, and boy, was it a drama. Dave's oxygen levels plummeted to 92 when we arrived at the hospital, and then, in a blink, his blood oxygen level went down to 62, turning my worst nightmare into a reality show I never signed up for. I had a quick talk with the doctor, He couldn't even assure me that Dave would be okay. "That's what we are trying to do," was all they could say. His words felt about as comforting as getting hugged by a cactus—definitely not the reassurance I was hoping for. That was when I knew I couldn't leave him there to fight this alone.

Just when I thought things couldn't get worse, my phone buzzed again. It was my daughter, reporting that Yssa—our resident immunocompromised family member—was running a fever. Great! As if juggling one medical crisis wasn't enough!

There I was, running around the hospital like a headless chicken, trying to admit Dave and get a room for him while coordinating Yssa's trip to the ER. It felt like I was starring in my own medical drama, minus the convenient commercial breaks.

When Yssa tested positive, too, I had to chuckle through my tears — not because it was funny, but because sometimes you just have to laugh at life's absurdity to keep you from going crazy.

Through it all, my heart was a rollercoaster of emotions— fear gripping me one moment, hope buoying me the next. I oscillated between feeling like a superhero mom and a helpless spectator in my family's health crisis. But in those quiet moments between the chaos, I found a strength I never knew I had, fueled by an unwavering love for my family and an adrenaline-powered determination to see us all through this nightmare.

Knowing Dave's condition was grave, doctors labelling his condition as Severe, and now that Yssa was going in, too, I decided to check myself into the COVID wing voluntarily against the hospital's policy. After getting my two other daughters' reluctant permission and fearful blessing (and probably a silent prayer that their mother hadn't completely lost her marbles), I requested (more like begged) the hospital to allow me to enter so I could take care of them full-time. They wouldn't allow me to admit them to a big room so we could all be together, so I braced myself for the long road of seeing both of them through this in separate rooms. Thankfully, they did manage to place Dave and Yssa just three doors apart. It was like a twisted game of musical rooms, and I was the player bouncing between them.

After signing the waiver and agreeing that once I go in, I cannot leave till both are healed and I passed a COVID test myself, I took a deep breath and put all our fates in God's hands…

My hospital day-to-days seem hazy now, like a movie, I replayed in my head like I wasn't in it. Those days blurred together like a fever dream — appropriate, given the circumstances. I floated through them in an out-of-body experience, smiling and pretending it was just another day at the beach… if the beach were filled with beeping machines and the constant smell of disinfectant.

My constant companions? An N95 mask and a face shield became more a part of me than my own skin. For eight days straight, these were my ride-or-die accessories. I NEVER took those off except during meal times that turned into a bizarre game of "how fast can you shove food in your mouth without breathing". I'd lift my shield, crack open my mask on one side, and perform a culinary magic trick—making empanadas and siopaos disappear in 10 seconds flat. It was like a one-woman eating contest, but instead of glory, the prize was just enough energy to keep going. And I did that facing the hospital door and farthest away from my patients who were both unmasked this whole time, just to lessen my already humongous risk of getting infected simply by being in that room with them 24/7.

Even showering became an Olympic sport. I would take a shower with that mask on and wait until the last moment to take it off to quickly wash my face, then slap on a fresh mask faster than you can say "hand sanitizer." It was a comedy routine without an audience.

And speaking of routines, while my insides were doing backflips in a nervous frenzy, my two patients seemed blissfully cocooned in their miracle bubble— their oxygen tubes looped around their necks like the latest designer trend, their faces serene as they breathed in life-saving air. Thankfully too, they hadn't lost their appetites, so every meal delivered from various restaurants courtesy of family worrying sick over us, was a delightful feast for them. Meanwhile, I was left to munch on whatever finger food I could shove, chew, and swallow in 60 seconds—all while hidden behind my mask like a ninja on a snack mission.

It was almost…surreal.

Here I was, my heart racing like a jackrabbit, my palms slick with sweat, while they lounged in their medical couture, oblivious to the storm brewing inside me. But that's the thing about chaos: it's always someone else's accessory.

Determined to keep their spirits high and their bodies in COVID-fighting form, I dove into research and crafted their daily routines. I transformed into their animated Zumba instructor, leading gentle workouts that had them giggling. I channeled my inner yoga coach, guiding stretches while ensuring they soaked up some sun by the window. And let's not forget the "turnover" sessions, like pancake flipping, where I helped them lie on their bellies to protect their lungs.

It was a chaotic mix of exercise and laughter, and though I sometimes felt like a circus act, I was all in for keeping the mood light in our little hospital haven. Anything to keep my beloved patients afloat while I battled my own fears! Through it all, I clung to hope and humor like a life raft in this sea of uncertainty. Because sometimes, when life hands you a pandemic, you've got to laugh to keep from crying—even if no one can see your smile behind the mask.

The first three days unfolded like a tense drama, filled with a blend of anxious hope and stark reality as the doctors administered the first round of antivirals. Each time they entered the room in their full PPE gear, it felt like a scene from a horror film—my heart sank with every update that Dave wasn't responding positively to the meds and that his severe COVID was worsening. Those words were painful reminders of just how real and terrifying our situation had become. All the while, Dave didn't feel too sick despite his worsening scans. He felt okay as long as my continuous supply of smiles and positive energy kept coming. I'll always be grateful for that miracle, believing it saved him from physically spiraling down as quickly as his lab results showed.

But on my end, each day brought a fresh wave of dread as the doctors conducted their relentless blood draws and X-ray scans. The anticipation of those results was like waiting for a storm to break, and it never got easier.

To make matters worse, Yssa was grappling with her own battle. After one particularly alarming lab result, the doctors determined she needed a blood transfusion; her anemia had reached a dangerously low level.

At that moment, I felt like I was caught in a whirlwind, darting between rooms, juggling conversations with doctors for each patient. My heart raced as I struggled to keep my emotions in check. I didn't know how to feel— my mind was a chaotic mix of fear and determination. All I wanted was for them to pull through this ordeal and, by some miracle, for me to emerge COVID-free as well so I could leave the hospital with them and continue getting them through their recovery.

By the third day, the Infectious Disease and Pulmonary doctors arrived with grave expressions, declaring they had no choice but to try another medication because nothing else was working—this was their last recourse.

My heart raced as I crossed my fingers and wished on every lucky star I could think of, praying fervently that this final hope would work. It was a moment suspended in time, where every second felt like an eternity filled with fear and desperation.

As I sat there, the weight of uncertainty pressed heavily on me. By this time, I had lost so much weight from stress and the meager food intake that my clothes hung loosely on me, and the tops of my ears were raw from wearing a face shield 24/7. The thought of losing Dave or Yssa was unbearable, and the stakes had never been higher; I barely noticed that I was starting to lose my voice from wearing my thick mask all day. Each passing hour felt like a rollercoaster through a nightmare, with hope flickering like a fragile candle in a storm. I clung to that flicker, determined to keep it alive as we faced this battle together.

On one of those hospital nights, the kind that blurs into the next, I caught a glimpse of something familiar through the window overlooking the parking lot. My heart skipped a beat as I squinted into the dim light —it was Yanna, standing by my car. For a moment, I froze, overwhelmed by the sight of her. Then, like a child desperate for attention, I climbed onto a chair and started waving wildly, my hands flailing against the glass, silently willing her to look up.

And then it happened. By some miracle, she glanced upward and saw me — her mother, dancing like a fool behind a lit hospital window. Her face broke into recognition, and in that instant, I felt the dam of my emotions burst. Tears streamed down my face as I stared at my daughter from my 5th floor window — the one who had been holding our household together in my absence, braving her fears while keeping everything afloat.

I grabbed my phone and called her, barely able to speak through my sobs. On the other end of the line, she couldn't hold back either. We both collapsed into wails— her fear, my longing, the weight of being apart.

Even as she drove home, she called me again on video. The screen lit up with her tear-streaked face, her whimpering so raw it shattered me all over again. There are no words to describe how heart-wrenching it was to see her like that — to feel her pain and know that all I wanted was to hold her but couldn't. It was love and longing wrapped in helplessness… there are no words for that kind of ache…

But just when it felt like hope was slipping away, redemption arrived, and we got our miracle. Dave began to improve, and Yssa's condition stabilized. The dark cloud that had enveloped us finally lifted, allowing a glimmer of light to shine through. Each day, the doctors entered the room with smiles that grew wider, and finally, we received the news we had been waiting for: they could go home.

And then, suddenly, all eyes turned to me. In that charged moment, I felt an unsettling certainty that I wouldn't be leaving the hospital with them. It was as if everyone silently accepted that I would be the one left behind, destined to confront my own battle with COVID-19 after being exposed for so long. I must admit, I had resigned myself to that fate.

So when the day finally came, and my swab results were revealed, the air crackled with tension. We were all stunned to discover that I was negative! In that instant, it felt like the universe had thrown me an unexpected lifeline, my own share of this miracle. It was as if the universe whispered a reminder that I still mattered, and in all the tension and worry over Dave and Yssa, it felt as if I was somehow lost in the shadows, yet I wasn't forgotten.

After a long drive home, with my two patients seated behind me in the passenger row (I still had to take precautions since I was told I could still catch COVID from them), I finally stepped into my own room. I could finally sleep in a bed!

Peeling off the plastic face shield and mask that had practically become a second skin, I felt an overwhelming wave of freedom and relief—emotions I hadn't realized I'd been craving so desperately during our time in the hospital. For the first time in what felt like forever, I felt the wind on my bare face and took a deep, unmasked breath. It was a moment of pure, simple joy—a reminder of how much we take for granted.

But that joy was short-lived. As I dialed my two other daughters, eager to share the update and see their faces on the screen, I heaved a deep, loud sigh of relief—only to discover no sound came out. My voice was gone!

It took me a moment to realize that my voice had retreated into my throat. I had to end the video call before anyone answered, giving myself a chance to coax my voice back slowly. Thankfully, it returned, but speaking felt labored for weeks and even months afterward. It took so much effort just to project my voice loud enough to be heard, probably due to my prolonged mask-wearing during our time in the hospital.

To this day, my strong, steady teacher's voice isn't how it once was. It's softer, weaker, as if it carries the weight of everything we endured. But even so, I would give it up a thousand times over for the miracles we were granted. Some sacrifices leave scars, but this one is a mark I carry with gratitude.

Each breath I take, each joy I see,
A well of peace awakens in me.
Through every trial, love shines bright,
Guiding my heart with endless light.

Each breath I take, each joy I see,
Gratitude grows and strengthens me.
In every moment, through dark or fair,
I find my strength in the love I bear.

Each breath I take, each joy I see,
Reminds me of all that life can be.
With open arms, I embrace the day.
Gratitude lights my path and way.

With each breath I take and joy I see,
Gratitude lives and sets me free.
With every inhale, I feel His grace,
Life's precious gift in this sacred space.

Chapter 10

One of life's greatest lessons is to move on. Through every joy and sorrow, every triumph and fear, we come to understand that it is all fleeting. So, we let go and embrace what lies ahead, for nothing lasts, only the possibilities of what comes next.

One painful yet victorious milestone down, and more on the way! In this wild ride called life, we discover a harsh truth: nothing lasts — not even those blissful moments, no matter how tightly we cling to them. So, we must learn to create and seek out new joys. After all, as long as you wake up to a brand-new day, you've got the chance to make more memories—so grab it! Life's too short not to chase the next happy moment, even if it means tripping over a few hurdles along the way!

Maybe it was a culmination of all the uphill battles, or maybe it was the fact that I just turned 50 and suddenly found myself questioning who I wanted to be in this next set of life chapters. I know— so dramatic! Have you met me? But who has time for all that sentimental soul-searching when there's cake to eat and new adventures to chase? If turning 50 means overthinking everything, at least I'm doing it with a laugh... and maybe a second slice of cake!

Turning half a century old has given me the gift of seeing myself. Now, I embrace each day with curiosity and look forward to daily discovery, knowing it won't always be sunshine and rainbows. Getting older has freed me from the pressure of Keeping up ... to be faster, stronger, brighter and just all around better than anyone else. For me, life is now about the challenge of Doing Me and getting better at it. I have a healthier respect for my limits so I can defy their constraints or move past them.

And since I'm the reigning queen of arduous goals and torturous dreams, would you really be shocked if I woke up one day and declared I'm going back to school after 25 long years? I surprise myself sometimes! It's like I've taken a masterclass in procrastination, only to realize that the final exam is still waiting for me. Who says you can't teach an old dog new tricks—or at least remind it how to fetch a diploma?

I decided to enroll in a Doctorate in Management course majoring in Leadership and Organization! I'm determined that my headstone will read "Dr. Mayette L. Pastrano." What's 3 years of studying and fumbling through the maze of learning to learn again while my brain has already started to mimic dementia symptoms!

Navigating the world of technology as the oldest student in a class full of tech-savvy classmates has been quite the challenge! Armed only with my outdated MS Word skills and rusty PowerPoint abilities, I feel like I've hit the reset button on my hard-earned confidence, which took 50 years to build. Holy Macanoly, this is hard! It's like showing up to a marathon in flip-flops while everyone else is sprinting in high-tech running shoes. But if I can survive this digital jungle, I can tackle anything — just pass me the coffee and a few tutorials!

I'll never forget the first time I had to do an oral report and share my screen. I had absolutely no clue how to do it! I was so nervous, fumbling around and sweating bullets —or was that just a full-blown menopausal hot flash kicking in? Honestly, who could tell? I felt like I was auditioning for a new reality show called Tech Fails:

Senior Edition. By the time I finally figured it out, I was ready to throw my laptop out the window and join a yoga retreat — preferably one with air conditioning! And I hadn't even started my report yet!

Fast forward two years, and just as I finally started feeling like I had this whole grad school thing under control, the last term hit. And what did I do? In a glorious act of self-sabotage, I decided to write a qualitative dissertation! Why? Who knows — maybe I wanted to spice things up, or maybe I just enjoy torturing myself. While my classmates and professors raised their eyebrows at my choice, I thought it would be a breeze—easy peasy … wrong!

Little did I know, I was about to learn the intricacies of stress management, complete with grilling sessions and all-nighters that nearly drove me to tears. I found myself knee-deep in endless interviews, trapped in overtime writing marathons, and drowning in enough rewrites to make my laptop scream for mercy. Cue the dramatic late-night breakdowns fueled by a dangerous mix of soda, coffee, and downright dread. By the end, I wasn't just researching — I was in full survival mode! It turns out "qualitative" is just fancy academic speak for "Welcome to the Hunger Games of dissertations!" May the odds be ever in my favor, because I definitely needed them!

To make this painful storytelling bearable, let me cut to the chase: I made it! Yoo-hoo! My oral defense and dissertation not only earned me a perfect grade but also filled my family with so much love and pride that it overshadowed any perfect grade any day (though, let's be real, the grade was a nice bonus).

Let me put on my doctorate hat and strike a serious pose for just a bit. My research culminated in the Two-Way Tactic Workspace Optimization (TWO) Model, a theoretical framework forged in the crucible of countless sleepless nights and an anxiety-driven writing frenzy. This model underscores the vital connection between a serene and optimized workspace and success in the architectural profession—a heartfelt nod to the world I share with my architect husband. Providing creative professionals with practical strategies to enhance their environments, this model is the result of all those rewrites, coffee crumble ice cream-fueled days, and caffeine-powered all-nighters. It's safe to say I'm beyond proud that it contributes something meaningful to the field!

To top it all off, I was assigned to deliver a thank-you speech on behalf of the graduating class of 2024 during our graduation ceremony; honored and thrilled, I said yes! Little did I know, graduation practice held a surprise even bigger than surviving my dissertation: I received the highest award in the entire university, Meritimus Gold! Talk about a grand slam with a cherry on top of a mountain of whipped cream! All the sacrifices, the physical toll, and analysis paralysis crises of the last three years culminated in the most dazzling, rainbow-sprinkled, heart-bursting gift imaginable. It was pure, unadulterated joy!

This journey wasn't just about finding my footing again; it was about giving back to my academic parents in a way they'd truly cherish. Forget the cliché "World's Best" mugs — I gifted them a dissertation, the ultimate nerd-standing ovation. Speaking their love language—academic achievement—I finally showed them the depth of my love and gratitude. While I spent weeks leading up to my defense feeling like a contestant on Survivor: Dissertation Edition, battling stress and caffeine withdrawals, the real prize was seeing their pride and knowing I'd honored everything they'd poured into me. That's a feeling worth every sleepless night.

Now that those sleepless writing marathons are just a blurry memory, I still can't believe I managed to wedge this enormous feat into my already overflowing life. There are moments when I realize I've somehow conquered my ridiculously impossible To-Do list in a mere 24 hours that I stop, breathless with inspired disbelief. The only explanation for me? God, in His infinite grace, slipped in a few extra hours into my day.

In those moments, I feel overwhelmingly blessed and loved, knowing He gifts me with the most impossible of miracles each and every day. It never fails to flood my soul with a surge of pure joy, sweeping away all the stress and the dark clouds of near-despair that threaten to consume me when battling life's relentless storms. Milestone after milestone, I stand in awe, deeply humbled and forever grateful, knowing I am fiercely loved, even in my most undeserving and difficult moments. It's a breathtaking, unbelievable, and profoundly moving miracle.

A Midlife Anthem for the Unlikely Scholar

I woke up at dawn, with a deadline to meet,
My joints creaked in protest, my brain
skipped a beat.
I'm older than my peers, but I still don't
know the drill—
Just a senior citizen, back in school to fulfill.

I'm a graduate, but still lost in the haze,
A midlife crisis wrapped in a diploma's daze.
I survived Google Classroom, the essays, the
stress,
But my sanity is still one big mess!

I'll trade my diploma for a rocking chair,
And hope my newfound wisdom follows me
there.
I'm too old for this, but I did it with pride,
A midlife student, surfing seniorhood's tide.

So here's to the midlife scholar,
We may be old, but we've raised the bar,
For those of us who dare to reinvent
Our stories will inspire—
long after we're spent!

Chapter 11

Sometimes, you need to lose something (even two) to gain back your whole self. So here's to all that we've lost, because perhaps, your best self starts with a shattered fall, so you can finally make that defiant climb.

As you've probably gathered by now, my life is a hilarious tug-of-war between my inner thrill-seeker and the nerdy bookworm screaming to be set free. So, naturally, after a deep dive into the academic abyss, I unintentionally, but totally in character, decided I needed an outdoor adventure, pronto! For ages, my youngest daughter and I had been dreaming of getting inked by the oldest tribal tattoo artist in the Philippines. What could possibly go wrong? (Spoiler alert: probably everything, but that's what makes it a great story!)

Tia and I plotted a pilgrimage to see Apo Whang-Od, the then 104-year-old queen of "mambabatok" tattooing from the Butbut tribe. In a world rich with tradition, Whang-Od was a straight-up legend. This woman wasn't just talented; she was exceptional, becoming the first woman ever allowed to learn the sacred art of traditional hand-tapped tattooing, a skill usually hogged by the tribal dudes. She fearlessly inked Butbut warriors back in the day (before headhunting became a major faux pas). And as if that weren't enough, she flipped tradition the bird again by choosing only female apprentices, turning Kalinga history on its head. Talk about a badass! And of course, we needed her badassery permanently inked on our skin. After all, who wouldn't want a little Whang-Od magic to remind them they can conquer anything?

And so, the saga begins... but hold on, this isn't just a mother-daughter tattoo trip! Of course, what else would you expect from me, the queen of dramatic milestone torture? Anyway, let's dive in, shall we?

Since Apo's village isn't exactly a hop, skip, and jump from civilization (think "middle of nowhere, accessible only by foot"), we wisely booked a guide. Getting lost and missing our chance to meet a living legend? Hard pass. Fresh off the plane from Cebu, we beelined to the mall for our rendezvous, planning a pre-hike feast and movie. We were rocking backpacks stuffed with gear for a weekend in the wilderness. And then there was me, blissfully sporting flip-flops as I dashed for cinema snacks, convinced my feet deserved a "last supper" before being imprisoned in hiking boots for two days. Famous last words, people, famous last words!

From the cinema's plush floor, I sashayed—or rather, waddled—towards the stairs, dreaming of food stalls. But on that fateful day in November 2022, my flip-flops staged a coup. One minute, I was upright; the next, I was starring in a live-action stunt show, careening down the stairs like a bowling ball gone rogue! Mountain trek survival skills kicked in (sort of). I clung to balance for a few steps (no handrail, naturally!), but gravity, that cruel mistress, had other plans. Assisted by the added weight of my backpack, I accelerated into a human rollercoaster, halfway down the staircase looking like I was auditioning for a superhero movie. Seriously, it was amazing I'd made it that far without falling. I remembered how we were taught to slide down scree in Morocco. That skill actually helped, and for a glorious moment, I thought, "I might actually nail this!"

I clung to my balance for as long as humanly possible until, two-thirds of the way down, I realized the inevitable: I was going down hard. I remember the seemingly slo-mo descent, the wide-eyed, horrified faces of onlookers witnessing my stunt, and a surprisingly calm inner voice that whispered, "Okay, genius, time to strategize!" The only thing I could do at this point was plan my fall with minimal damage. I braced myself for impact, silently commanding my reflexes not to break my fall with my limbs, lest I end up with a souvenir collection of broken bones. As I prepared for the dive, I managed to twist my body sideways, aiming to land on my left side. "Anything but my face or my back!" I mentally screamed, picturing a neck-snapping disaster. My goal: protect my spine and neck and avoid any joint-wrenching sprains. Miraculously, I landed on my intended side, the left side of my arm was supposed to break my fall. But the speed and momentum were brutal. My head slammed into the unforgiving ground, my mouth heroically sacrificing itself as a brake on the edge of the last few steps. Instant dental apocalypse: my teeth surrendered, roots and all, cascading down the steps.

When my spectacular tumble finally screeched to a halt, my first instinct was to perform a mental body audit without moving a muscle. My initial thought? "Well, I think I stuck that landing-ish! No broken neck, so that's a win, right? Haha." Gingerly, I sat up. By this time, a squadron of security guards had descended upon me, their faces a mask of bewildered panic, possibly more rattled than I was. They seemed to freeze mid-stride, hovering over me and repeatedly asking if I was alright. Classic security guard protocol, I suppose. So, I took matters into my own hands and conducted my own damage assessment. Arms moving? Check. Legs still attached and moving? Check. No imminent fainting? Check. Definitely in shock, but functioning enough to ensure I wasn't, you know, dying. Looking back, the whole scene was pure comedy.

There I was, meticulously prodding and poking myself, checking for broken bits, while a gaggle of security guards stared in awe and terror. One was even stroking my head like I was his daughter who'd just wiped out on her bike. Red carpet? Nope, just a mall staircase and gravity. My inner DJ went rogue, blasting the "Mission: Impossible" theme on elevator-music repeat as the guards and I starred in: "Stairway to...Ouch."

Now, let's see... Ten minutes. That's all it had been since I left my daughter at the ticket booth, but in my world, an actual eternity had passed. Post-body scan, I realized I was...moist. Turns out, it was blood gushing from my demolished mouth. Ah, that explains the zombie-apocalypse stares from the guards! Not only had I lost two of my front teeth (RIP, my pearly whites), my upper lip had split open, leaving a gaping, gruesome slit that showcased the carnage. Every time I spoke, the cut flapped open and shut like some grotesque puppet show. Blood. Just. Kept. Flowing. I croaked out a request for ice and something I could apply pressure with, and the guards returned, faces still etched with shock, bearing... three refrigerator ice cubes wrapped in a tissue. Five-star first aid, woohoo!

Reality hit me. First thought: "Shoot, can I even hike to the village now without my two front teeth?" Then: "Tia! I need to call her before she buys those tickets!" When I did, I probably sounded like I'd just embarrassingly tripped over my own feet. I even laughed (probably gurgled) to keep her from panicking and attempting her own staircase dive. For a second, she didn't even believe I'd had an actual accident. But when she arrived and saw me bloodied and slumped on the stairs, her face said it all. Turns out, my "little slip" was a Code Red situation. One look, a perfunctory "You okay?" and BAM! Superhero Tia emerged, alerting the family back home, speed-dialing a doctor to wait for us at the hospital, and summoning an ambulance.

The ER stay was a masterclass in waiting. Apparently, walking and talking downgrades your "emergency" status. So, while family and friends flooded my phone with concerned calls, I tried cheering up my daughter with jokes (bad idea). She finally begged me to stop smiling, terrified my lip-slit would rip wider! Poor child. Weekend trek ruined, now she's stuck babysitting a bloody, toothless wonder in the ER. Talk about a vacation upgrade. NOT!

Once the scan-o-rama (X-rays, the whole shebang) and lalapalooza (blood draws, the works) were done, it was finally stitching time. Knowing my pain tolerance is legendary (read: I'm stubborn and stupid), Tia stationed herself beside me, a one-woman pain barometer. She watched my body language like a hawk: the barely perceptible shivers, the curled toes, the rogue tears escaping against my will. One look at the barely veiled torture, and she'd roar, "More anesthesia, STAT! This woman is about to spontaneously combust from stoicism!" Turns out, even superhero moms need a translator...and a whole lotta drugs.

The following days were a blur of pain, punctuated by more pain. Eating? A cruel joke! With my lip stitched like a Frankenstein experiment, food had to navigate the good side of my mouth (you know, aside from the toothless chasm on the other). Even soup was a challenge, dribbling out the gaping hole like a leaky faucet.

Forget happily ever after; that face-plant launched a year-long saga of four surgeries, bone grafts, and tooth-replacement hell. I knew it was a marathon, but I wasn't about to wait a year to reclaim my narrative! Two months post-staircase swan dive, sporting temporary dentures, my daughter and I boarded that same flight, endured a 12-hour drive, and trekked to Apo Whang-Od's village in pitch-black darkness. Because I refused to bury my lost teeth and endure all that pain for absolutely nothing.

It felt like a pilgrimage, a brutal rite of passage, like Moses parting the Red Sea. I entered broken and injured, yet emerged remarkably whole, even if my two front teeth are now just stylishly faux! Now, my kids get twitchy when I approach stairs, clearly more traumatized for me than I actually am. If you ask me today if I fear any staircase, my answer is a resounding "No." And that, my friends, is nothing short of a miracle. It's a reminder that even a face-plant can lead to redemption.

Better shoes next time, though. Definitely better shoes.

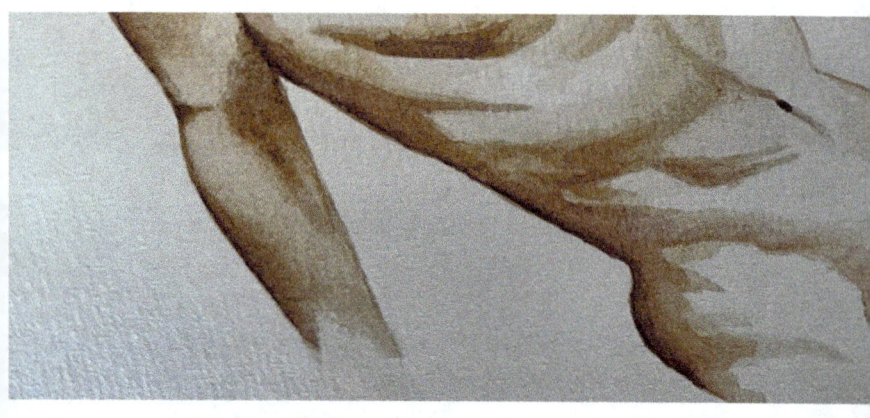

The tooth fairy came for me, decades late—
She left a note: 'Next time,
better shoes, mate.'
I laughed with a gap-toothed grin,
And vowed to heal from the fall's bitter spin.
For even a face-plant can birth a hero's tale,
Where scars are badges,
and dentures prevail.

Chapter 12

Fate doesn't steal from us to weaken,
but to unburden. Releasing the past lets
us glimpse a future, however daunting.
Perhaps diminished, we gain space for
unforeseen strength to flourish. And
that is a story worth telling.

By now, you know I thrive on contradiction – defying illness with trapeze acts. But this unwell chapter isn't just a chapter; it's a freakin' saga. From day one, I've been a walking petri dish! I had every virus and childhood sickness even before I could get the immunization shots for it! Name it, I had it all! But the minute I could strong-arm my health, I did! I morphed into an enthusiastic fitness newbie. Sports, healthy-ish eating, the works! Because let's face it, sick days aren't cute when you're paying the bills.

Miraculously, I've kept things in check. Even fueled by fat, cake and ice cream binges, my labs stayed stubbornly normal (Thank you, Universe!). I figured I'd earned a lifetime pass... then menopause sashayed in, stage left, wearing a sequined jumpsuit and wielding a flaming torch.

Never, ever did I imagine menopause would body-slam me so hard. I was far too smug, convinced I wouldn't be one of those women fanning themselves and lamenting the cruelties of aging. When my period got "erratic" (translation: hit-or-miss) in my mid-40s, I thought, "Ha! Is that all you got, menopause? Child's play!"

Flash forward, the "erratic" bleeding escalated to a full-blown waterfall. Thinking it was just my period's dramatic exit, I ignored it... I casually mentioned my superpower of bloodletting, and my doctor raised an eyebrow and said, "No way, José, that ain't menopause!" Cue the biopsy. Turns out, there were abnormal readings in my uterus. "Nothing scary," she said. So maybe, it's like Stage 0? Hmmm, what's with Stage Zero? Is that like winning a participation trophy in the Cancer Olympics?

It felt like a cosmic punchline! After a lifetime as a sickly underdog, I finally win at health, only for my uterus to throw a rave with questionable cells as the headliners.

So much for aging gracefully. Turns out, menopause wasn't going to be a gentle sunset. It was shaping up to be a glitter-cannon-fueled hormonal circus.

And so, this chapter – less beautiful head and all – barges in. I was slathered in hormones for months to quell a uterine rebellion, but my uterus was clearly on strike. So, options were laid out: since I was undeniably past my child-bearing years (unless a miracle involving a very confused stork happened), and my menopause journey didn't seem to be ending anytime soon, my doctor gently suggested the sensible option of a total hysterectomy. Snip, snip, and sayonara, uterus!

And so, we scheduled the eviction. But, because I'm me, I couldn't just waltz calmly into the operating room. Oh no. I had a trip scheduled! Plus, I was in training for a bike race! I pictured myself, post-surgery, a sad little potato on the couch while everyone else was conquering hills and breathing in fresh, non-hospital air. So, I batted my eyelashes (okay, maybe I just pleaded dramatically), and requested a delay. "Just a month or so, pretty please?" My OB, bless her heart, saw my desperation and graciously conceded.

Little did we know, a few weeks after, COVID would crash the party in a hazmat suit and wrecking ball in tow. My uterus might have been plotting a mutiny, but the universe unleashed a full-scale pandemic. Talk about timing! Is my life a comedy or a tragedy? Asking for a friend.

Since lopping out my uterus wasn't exactly front-line pandemic triage, my doctor wisely advised we wait until hospitals were less … apocalyptic. So, there I was, swimming in hormone meds, trying to negotiate a ceasefire with my rebellious uterus, hoping to convince it that blowing up my lady parts wasn't the answer. All while waiting for COVID to get bored of terrorizing the planet. It was like living in a darkly comedic medical drama, where the fate of my reproductive system hung in the balance while the world imploded. I spent my days Googling symptoms (a terrible idea, always), mainlining herbal teas promising hormonal harmony, and mentally composing strongly worded letters to my uterus. " Can't you just chill? The world is ending! Now is not the time for a uterine uprising!"

Cutting to the chase, somewhere amidst the chaos, my focus shifted. I went from obsessively monitoring my insides to… just… not caring anymore! Whether it was divine intervention, a cosmic distraction putting all those other life-or-death issues in my path, or whether my uterus simply got bored and decided to stage its rebellion elsewhere, I'll never know. The daily drama faded into the background noise of a world gone mad. Long story short, no hysterectomy. It just... suddenly... didn't seem important anymore.

The irony wasn't lost on me: I'd spent months battling my body, only to have the world throw a pandemic at me and make the whole uterine kerfuffle seem utterly insignificant. But hey, this story actually got a happy ending! Thank the heavens – and maybe a slightly disgruntled uterus! Who knew the secret to hormonal harmony was a global crisis? Go figure.

But Madame Menopause was never one to be outdone by a pesky pandemic and a temporarily subdued uterus. Oh no, she was just biding her time, and planning her grand entrance. Just when my uterus decided to play nice, BAM! Ten years after menopause first waltzed into my life, she unleashed her full, unadulterated fury. Suddenly, my whole body hurt... to the bone! I swear, I felt like I had bone cancer or something equally terrifying. Literally, from the top of my head to the soles of my feet, every slow, agonizing step felt like walking on shards of glass. At first, I blamed it on dissertation-fueled sleepless nights. But even after hibernating like a grumpy bear, it still felt like I hadn't slept a wink!

Then the Great Tummy Conspiracy. I'd always had a relatively flat stomach. Even after ballooning to whale-like proportions during three pregnancies, hitting almost 200 pounds, my tummy remained stubbornly, almost defiantly, flat-ish. But now? Even with a measly five pounds of extra weight, it looked like my stomach was auditioning to be a basketball. My weight was on a one-way trip to higher numbers! Bloating, zombie attacks, Coke-demanding mood swings, and the soul-crushing desperation of control-freak me. I felt helpless, swallowed whole by a monstrous, hormonal sea of misery, swimming harder only to glimpse the distant shore. Madame Menopause had arrived, and she was not messing around.

Navigating this life stage had been less a gentle cruise and more a tumultuous shipwreck. Every day brought a fresh assault of aches, pains, and downright weird changes that rippled through my body, mind, and what was left of my rapidly dwindling sanity. It was a disheartening, overwhelming, and frankly rude witness to the gradual erosion of what once was. It felt like watching a slow-motion film of my former self disintegrating.

I hadn't biked in two years, thanks to my traitorous shoulders demanding not one, but two surgeries, one on each side! Not to mention the creeping mental fog and the fading physical reflexes – it felt like my brain was running on dial-up while my body was stuck in slow-mo. The loss wasn't just physical; it was a deep, aching emotional grief for the vitality, strength, and mental clarity slipping away.

But damn it, I'm a stubborn optimist! A believer in the power of positive thinking, even when my hormones are plotting my demise. So, one day, I woke up, fueled by a potent cocktail of fury and desperation, and decided: enough is enough!

This wasn't going to be a silent, defeated surrender. I gathered courage, took a deep breath (hoping I wouldn't burst into flames from the resulting hot flash), and did what any self-respecting modern woman would do: I took to Instagram. That's right, I declared war on the Big M in a carefully crafted post, complete with inspirational hashtags and a slightly blurry artsy selfie. Because what's a good old-fashioned declaration of war without a carefully curated social media campaign?

I made my battle cry against the Big M as public and loud as I could, so I couldn't chicken out! No turning back now, folks! In my September 1, 2024 post (mark your calendars, it's a day that will live in infamy!), I shouted my call to arms. Not a cry for help; but a promise: I refuse to let this phase define me or diminish my spirit. No quiet surrender but a defiant battle for my own damn life! And in that very public statement, I held myself accountable to all who read my post. This was a battle, and I was just getting started. Let the games begin!

Post-Instagram update: no heroic victory … just yet. Rome wasn't built in a day, and a rebellious uterus isn't subdued with a single motivational quote, apparently. But after trying Hormone Replacement Therapy (which, after a while, I realized my body wasn't exactly making friendship bracelets with), a month-long colon cleanse (desperate times!), and other experimental strategies … I've got a handle on my meno-belly! For now, at least! And, miracle of miracles, I've lost ten glorious pounds!

It's been almost a year since my period graced me with its unmistakable presence (or rather, absence), so I'm cautiously hopeful that I can finally declare victory and say, "I've menopaused!" Maybe all this will finally be over. If this road is still long and winding, I'm okay with it. I've learned to battle it out as graciously and gracefully as I can, eye-twitches and muttered curses directed at my ovaries included. For now, I'm still at war, but it's looking a whole lot more peaceful on the home front.

This journey has been a raw, relentless reckoning, a painful stripping away of the self I thought I knew. But in the midst of the struggle, I've learned that life sometimes takes from us not to diminish, but to lighten our spirits, to free us from the weight of who we were so that we can somehow, impossibly, look forward to what is to come, even if it feels like being less than what we started with. Because maybe, just maybe, "less" is just making room for something new to bloom – something wiser, stronger, and infinitely more resilient. And maybe, just maybe, that's a victory worth fighting for.

The 12th Chapter Playbook: 10 Steps to Power Through the Pause

1. Embrace the Shift
How: Frame menopause as a natural transition, not a crisis. Celebrate the wisdom and confidence that comes with age.

2. Prioritize Self-Care Rituals
How: Make time for activities that nourish your mind, body, and soul — like meditation, baths, or hobbies, even shopping!

3. Stay Active with Joy
How: Engage in movement that feels fun, whether it's dancing, hiking, or yoga. Exercise boosts mood and energy.

4. Eat to Energize
How: Focus on nutrient-rich foods that support hormonal balance and overall health. Yes, chocolate can be one of those!

5. Laugh at the Chaos
How: Humor softens the edges of hot flashes and mood swings. Find the absurdity in it all even if you have to pee your way through the laughter!

6. Take a Road Trip with Friends
How: Celebrate freedom and friendship with a fun adventure.

7. Advocate for Your Needs
How: Speak up about your health, boundaries, and desires. Your voice matters ... you matter.

8. Connect with Your Tribe
How: Surround yourself with supportive friends, family, or community groups. Shared laughter and advice ease the journey.

9. Explore New Passions
How: Try a hobby, travel, or skill you've always wanted to pursue. Menopause is a time for reinvention.

10. Celebrate Your Resilience
How: Acknowledge your strength in navigating life's changes. You've got this!

Chapter 13

Life's a relentless carousel, isn't it?
Echoes of yesterday always return,
bruised or utterly transformed. But in
that inevitable reunion with our past
self, understanding dawns: even broken
pieces form a beautiful mosaic. The
circle, however altered, is finally whole.

Doesn't life always lead us back to the beginning, no matter how far we wander? Scars may mark the journey, and our reflection might be altered, yet a haunting familiarity lingers. In that destined return, a bittersweet wholeness emerges, a quiet understanding that even endings cradle new beginnings. In this winding path, I've discovered that some truths are etched into our being from the start. From the most profound depths of my soul, a certainty resonated: I was meant to be a mother!

From the day I vowed to marry by 21, life conspired to deliver me to that sacred place where my children bloomed into existence, and my true life began. Thirty years flew by in a whirlwind of audacious twists, heart-stopping turns, and utterly absurd adventures. Yet, every thread, no matter how tangled, somehow wove its way back to this: what I was always, undeniably, meant to be.

And now, as I look back, I realize that even the most ridiculous goals were just detours on the path to this moment – a moment that reminds me that life's greatest gifts often lie in the simplest truths.

Then came that unbidden moment, a heartbeat stretched into an eternity, where I stood breathless, confronting the reality that my little souls, the oxygen of my being, the reason my heart beat in rhythm, had taken flight without needing my permission or presence. Leaving me with the exquisite agony of confronting … myself.

All the hard-won victories, the soul-crushing defeats, the meaningful, and intentional sacrifices that later bloomed into a thousandfold reward for my weary soul, all the colossal mistakes that left indelible marks on my spirit and those that got crushed along the way, to my dismay and heartfelt regret … led me to this precipice where I felt, with a bone-deep certainty, that I no longer had a reason to exist.

Is it just me, or everyone else is predisposed to morph into walking telenovelas at every life milestone? Seriously, can't I just flip a switch to "stoic acceptance" instead of "full-blown existential crisis"? Why can't I just grab a sparkly pom-pom and join the damn parade, celebrating a lifetime mostly lived, culminating in the glorious freedom of having offsprings who no longer require my chauffeur services or my parental blessing to shake their groove thing when they're out with friends? Is it too much to ask to be just slightly less emotionally extra about this whole "empty nest" thing!?

So, at this point, I was down to one adult chickadee at home. One had flown the coop, hitched, and bought a townhouse pre-nuptial (smart cookie!). The other? Well, she chased her own North Star across the ocean, convinced the life she was meant to have, was waiting there – bless her adventurous soul. That move, of course, came with its own special brand of melodrama. The post airport drop-off was a dramatic affair – wailing, theatrical weeping, and possibly some pearl-clutching. What can I say, I'm a walking, talking emoji, the exaggerated kind.

After that initial tidal wave of emotions subsided, there were the usual ripples of highs and lows with having a loved one living roughly the distance of Pluto. But we adjusted to our long-distance life, mastering bittersweet video calls. Truth be told, I was almost nailing this "empty nest" thing, AGAIN…

So now I was rocking the "I AM FREE!" anthem, embracing my newfound days of … well, whatever the hell I wanted. I had resigned myself to the fact that I was too darn tired to keep playing the stay-at-home-Mama card. And so, I did my thing: plotting exotic (aka affordable) trips with the hubby, and embarking on a borderline obsessive quest for cheap non-invasive anti-aging gizmos, potions, and vitamins known to humankind. Let's face it, I'm hurtling towards 60 faster than a runaway train, and my new mission, should I choose to accept it, was to arrive at that milestone looking like I'd aged gracefully on a remote island, nourished by nothing but spinach smoothies and positive affirmations – naturally!

My days were a whirlwind of chores, YouTube gurus promising eternal youth, and office work with my husband-boss. It was a gloriously boring existence, but a spa day for my soul after years of exhilarating (and exhausting) chaos.

Was I, in my mid-50s, finally achieving that legendary "mellow" state – trading my Doc Martens for fuzzy slippers and plotting retirement with NASA-like precision? But, let's be real, my attempts at stoicism just made me crave Coke and ice cream more. I am even loving staying at home… all the time! The pandemic lockdowns turned me into a perpetual hibernating Mama Bear till now! So much so, that my kids staged interventions, urging me to find a life beyond the four walls I referred to as my Fortress of Solitude (and Laundry).

Here I was, a budding social hermit, proudly sporting my "I Survived Motherhood" badge. Yet, beneath the surface, a nagging feeling persisted – a sense that a part of me was lost, wandering aimlessly in the wilderness of my now nearly empty home.

My heart, once a vibrant canvas of motherhood, now felt faded and worn. But then, on Valentine's Day 2024, my married daughter, Yanna, burst into my morning, bearing gifts for my happy heart. My big babies never forget me on occasions like these; I was one lucky mama, indeed.

With a mischievous grin, she handed me a gift that would forever change my life – a pregnancy test, that most noble of pee-soaked artifacts, proudly displaying its life-altering verdict: "YES, WE'RE PREGNANT!" And in that instant, my soul roared back to life, shouting, "It's not time to slowly see your light flicker out just yet, Mama! The show is far from over!

Witnessing my daughter's new chapter unfold was like being reborn – reliving the joy of motherhood through her eyes. Seeing her radiate with the same unbridled joy I once felt filled me with overwhelming peace and contentment.

In the quiet moments between joyful shock and happy disbelief, I felt the universe whispering its secrets – that life will always be a tapestry of joy, love and new beginnings, each thread a poignant reminder of the unbreakable bond of family and love. As I watched my daughter step into the gentle light of motherhood, I felt my heart resonate with hers, our souls entwined in a dance of joy and wonder. It was no longer about my own journey; it was about witnessing her heart bloom with a love so pure, so unshakeable, that it transformed me forever.

In that moment, I knew I was exactly where I was meant to be – a grandmother, enveloped in purpose and belonging. It was a feeling of profound peace, a sense of coming full circle, knowing that I had lived a full life of love, laughter, and adventure, and now, I get to experience it all again through my child's eyes. Watching my daughter become a mother filled me with joy and gratitude. I was no longer just a grandmother; I was a guardian of memories, a keeper of traditions, and a source of love and wisdom for generations to come.

And thus, the tapestry of my years has reached its most beautiful moment, a culmination of love and adventure. I can feel this season of my life gently closing and the unfolding of another - a new journey of love, pain and radiant light. With her birth, a new generation of unstoppable, strong, independent women begins – a legacy that will carry on long after I'm gone. And I, her Lolli, am blessed to spend the remainder of my lifetime basking in the warmth of her presence, cherishing every moment as our hearts entwine in a dance of new beginnings.

As I look into the future, I see a bright horizon, lit by the promise of tomorrow, and my heart overflows with joy and anticipation for the adventures that await us.

And so, with a heart full of love and a soul at peace, I welcome this new chapter of my life, one that will be forever intertwined with the life of our new miracle... Adriana Rose.

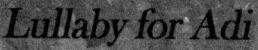

Lullaby for Adi

Sweet little Adi, don't you cry;
Lolli's gonna sing you this lullaby.
Hush, little one, and close your eyes;
I'm here so you can rest in peaceful skies.

As the world sleeps, let your worries fade,
In the warmth of my love, you'll never be
afraid.
Adventure awaits in the dreams that you
weave,
So drift off to slumber; it's time to believe.

Sweet dreams will find you with each passing
hour,
You're my little miracle, my blooming flower.
Rest now, dear Adi, let your spirit take flight;
Lolli will be here, through
the dark and the light.

About the Author

Mayette Lerin Pastrano - Wife, Mama of three, and Lolli to one (with room for more, definitely!). Part-time Graduate School Professor, Business Owner, Certified Public Accountant, Doctor in Management with a

Master's in Business Education degree and a passion for teaching that borders on obsession. Full time Chief Chaos Coordinator and House Manager wrangling kids, dogs, laundry and the occasional existential crisis.

A lifelong lover of life's messy beauty, she writes with humor and heart about the art of thriving—not just surviving—life's big shifts. Whether dissecting the absurdity of hot flashes or celebrating the quiet victories of motherhood, she believes that wisdom grows best in the garden of grit and grace.

When she's not grading papers, cycling or refereeing snack disputes, you'll find her scribbling notes, sipping tea, or plotting her next adventure. A firm believer that resilience is the best accessory, she's here to remind you that even the most chaotic chapters can be rewritten with courage and curiosity, and a really good sense of humor.

(P.S. She's still figuring out how to adult, but she's happy to share her notes.)

Special thanks to my daughter,
Tia for all the beautiful art used
in the book!